California Government and Politics Today

FOURTEENTH EDITION

Mona Field

Glendale Community College

PEARSON

Boston   Columbus   Indianapolis   New York   San Francisco
Upper Saddle River   Amsterdam   Cape Town   Dubai   London   Madrid
Milan   Munich   Paris   Montreal   Toronto   Delhi   Mexico City
São Paulo   Sydney   Hong Kong   Seoul   Singapore   Taipei   Tokyo

Executive Editor: Reid Hester
Editorial Assistant: Emily Sauerhoff
Executive Marketing Manager: Wendy Gordon
Production Project Manager: Clara Bartunek
Project Coordination, Text Design, and Electronic Page
    Makeup: Hemalatha, Integra Software Services Pvt. Ltd.
Cover Design Manager: Jayne Conte
Cover Designer: Suzanne Duda
Cover Art: © Chad Ehlers/Alamy Fotolia
Printer/Binder/Cover: Courier Companies

Library of Congress Cataloging-in-Publication Data
Field, Mona.
   California government and politics today / Mona Field.—Fourteenth ed.
     p. cm.
   Includes bibliographical references and index.
   ISBN-13: 978-0-205-25178-0
   ISBN-10: 0-205-25178-1
   1. California—Politics and government—1951-   I. Title.
JK8716.F54 2013
320.9794—dc23

                                                        2011048397

9 10 11—V092—15 14

ISBN 10:   0-205-25178-1
ISBN 13: 978-0-205-25178-0

> *For my many friends and colleagues who*
> *inspire me to learn more and do better.*
> MONA FIELD

Contents

Preface

Welcome to the Fourteenth Edition of *California Government and Politics Today*. After over 35 years in existence, this textbook's mission is still to explain California's ever-changing political situation in the context of social and economic trends. The focus remains on ethnic and cultural diversity, the global economy's impact on California (and vice versa), and the emphasis on political involvement as an essential component of achieving the California Dream.

NEW TO THIS EDITION

While the state is still an economic powerhouse, the current economic climate is the worst since the 1930s, and the long-term predicted population growth (50 million people by 2050) creates deep concerns about where and how everyone will live. This edition acknowledges the gloomy state of affairs in the Golden State, and reports on the economic downturn and political dysfunction that have so badly hurt California's people and its reputation. New details about ongoing public cutbacks as well as increasingly urgent dilemmas regarding energy supplies, educational opportunities, and political reform possibilities add depth to the basic information already in the text.

The new political districts for the legislature and Congress as well as the "top two" primary elections are explained, and recent actions such as the signing of the California DREAM Act and the appointment of former UC Berkeley professor Goodwin Liu to the state Supreme Court bring students up to date. A new focus in Chapter 14 on the two systems of public higher education (CSU and UC) helps students understand the governance and fiscal circumstances of our two public university systems. Other new and important information involves data from the most recent public opinion polls about the state and its future, much of it from the excellent work of the Public Policy Institute of California. As always, this text is designed to give students a broad background that enables them to understand, analyze, and interpret fast-changing events. To that end, and to engage students, the text includes interactive learning tools in each chapter that have been updated in this new edition.

Debating the Issues presents contrasting views of important political issues facing the state and can be used to spark classroom discussion. Each "Debating the Issues" box includes "Ask Yourself"—a brief question designed to stimulate thinking and research.

Compared to California provides unique insights about the political structures and processes of California by comparing them to the federal system, other states, and other nations.

Enjoying Media: Movies to See and Websites to Explore includes both documentaries and Hollywood fiction, as well as Websites that illuminate various aspects of California life.

ADDITIONAL LEARNING AIDS

The text still includes "Questions to Consider" at the end of each chapter. All of these tools can be used to stimulate class discussion or to develop themes for essays and term papers. The book continues to feature numerous updated charts and maps, a glossary (defining terms that appear in *italics* in the text), a section dedicated to "How to Communicate with Your Elected Officials," a bibliography for further reading, and a list of political organizations that students may wish to learn more about.

Students who want to reinforce their learning may take advantage of MySearchLab with Pearson eText. This book-specific website features a full, interactive eText; complete overviews of the entire writing and research process; and chapter-specific content such as learning objectives, quizzes, media, and flashcards to enrich learning and help students succeed.

For the benefit of instructors, a complete test bank is available.

ACKNOWLEDGMENTS

This edition has benefited from the input of colleagues from around the state, including Michael Bressler, Long Beach City College; Kathleen Holland, Los Angeles Pierce College; and Kimberly Naider, California State University–Sacramento. Thanks are also due to colleague Andra Verstraete from Glendale Community College, who always reminds me that the goal is a student-friendly textbook.

I thank everyone for their important input, which has enabled me to improve the book. I remain personally responsible for the final product, including its strengths and weaknesses. Further ideas and suggestions from colleagues are most welcome, so feel free to contact me directly with your comments.

As always, the goal remains to enlighten our students and help them achieve their share of the California Dream—in whatever form available.

MONA FIELD
mfield@glendale.edu

CHAPTER ONE

California Politics in Perspective

California is in the midst of a surprising transformation from a migration magnet that supplies its needs from outside the state to a more self-contained society that depends on its present members. We have become a land of settled and increasingly committed residents who share a future together.

—Dowell Myers, University of Southern California Demographer.

As Californians move into the second decade of the twenty-first century, there are deep concerns about the quality of life in the Golden State. Is California on the edge of a major decline, with public education, state parks, social services, and other government activities getting cut so severely that the future is jeopardized? Or is state government undergoing a much-needed "live within our means" correction?

If you ask Governor Jerry Brown and the Democrats in the legislature, it's the former. But the Republican minority in the legislature claims it is the latter. Both sides claim to have popular support, and given the state's red/blue divide, probably both are correct. California, despite having elected an all-Democratic executive branch, and having a huge Democratic majority in its legislature, still has a Republic core in the Central Valley, the Inland Empire, and most of the northeast counties. The Democratic coast and urban areas may have more people, but the minority Republicans still have a veto over any taxes.

As Californians go about their lives, many of them completely oblivious to the drama in the state capitol, the question remains: Will the current budget cause long-term damage to children, to college students, to the disabled, and to the parks and beaches that beautify the state?

Or will government do less and individuals have to pay more for their services? And what does the future hold for Californians if things continue as they are?

Ironically, with all its budget messes, California remains a world economic power: If California were a separate nation, it would rank in the top ten nations in gross domestic production (GDP). California still leads the nation in population, although growth is slowing for the first time in the state's history (see Table 1.1).

California is not alone among the states in suffering a severe economic downturn. The so-called Great Recession (2008–?), in which the state's unemployment rate rose to record levels,[1] only aggravates California's status as a *two-tier society*, in which the contrasts between "haves" and "have-nots" are even more noticeable. The springboard for new economic growth has yet to emerge from today's tough times

TABLE 1.1

California's Population: Growth Since Statehood

Year	Population
1850	92,597
1860	379,994
1870	560,247
1880	864,694
1890	1,213,398
1900	1,485,053
1910	2,377,549
1920	3,426,861
1930	5,677,251
1940	6,907,387
1950	10,586,223
1960	15,717,204
1970	19,971,069
1980	23,667,902
1990	31,400,000
2010	37,253,956
Projected 2020	45,821,900

Source: U.S. Census Bureau, State Department of Finance.

although some experts place hopes on activities such as alternative energy development, public *infrastructure* construction, and "public–private partnerships" to get people working again.

NATIONAL IMPACT: SETTING TRENDS FOR THE COUNTRY

At least in theory, based on the numbers, California remains among the most powerful states in the nation. The U.S. Census has repeatedly confirmed that California is first in population, and therefore has the most members in Congress. The state has 53 of the 435 members of the House of Representatives and 55 *electoral votes*, more than a fifth of the 270 necessary to elect a president. Even with the slim possibility of population decline ahead, the state will retain the largest congressional delegation, with Texas (32 seats) and New York (29 seats) far behind. One new element in the mix is the newly drawn Congressional districts (2011) that may result in some senior California congress members losing office in a national system where seniority is power.

Although having the most people should bring California the largest share of federal grants, funds, and contracts, the realities of Washington politics keep Californians sending more dollars to Washington, D.C., than they receive back in funds for state and local services. In 2002, California had over 12 percent of the nation's population, contributed over 14 percent of total federal taxes, and received back 11 percent of federal dollars sent to states and localities.[2]

COMPARED TO CALIFORNIA

POVERTY RATES IN CALIFORNIA AND THE NATION (2002, PERCENTAGES)

	California	Rest of United States
Poor	13.1	11.9
Low income	32.9	30.1
Middle income	51.3	56.7
Affluent	15.8	13.3

Source: Deborah Reed, "Recent Trends in Income and Poverty," *California Counts*, Public Policy Institute of California, Vol. 5, No. 3, February 2004, p. 9.

Think Critically: How do you feel about the poor? Who is responsible for helping those living in poverty? What is your role?

THE STATE AND ITS PEOPLE: POWER BLOCS IN CONFLICT

Like most Americans, Californians are impacted most directly by their state and local political systems. The state determines the grounds for divorce; traffic regulations; public college tuition fees; penalties for drug possession; and qualifications one needs to become a barber, psychologist, or lawyer. It establishes the amount of unemployment compensation, the location of highways, the subjects to be taught in school, and the rates to be charged by telephone, gas, and electric companies. Along with the local governments under its control, it regulates building construction, provides police and fire protection, and spends about 15 percent of the total value of goods and services produced by California residents.

The policy decisions made in these and other areas are influenced by the distribution of political power among various groups with competing needs and aspirations. Some of the power blocs reflect the same conflicts of interest that the nation experiences: labor vs. business; landlords vs. tenants; and environmentalists vs. oil companies. But, as in so many things, these battles are fought on a grander scale in California. With its incredibly complex array of local governments, including over 3,400 *special districts* to provide everything from street lights to flood control, California's political system almost defies understanding. No wonder that voters have shown their overall mistrust of elected officials and turned to *ballot initiatives* to make new laws and even to amend the state constitution.

These ballot initiatives, or *propositions*, deal with everything from juvenile crime to educational policy, from Indian gaming rights to the ever-present insurance industry issues. While political experts despise the use of initiatives to set public policy, ballot measures are big business. Virtually all propositions are placed on the ballot by *special-interest groups*, either organizations or wealthy individuals. Profitable petition-gathering companies charge several dollars per signature to get issues on the ballot. The outcome of these initiative battles usually depends on such factors as money, media, and the public mood.

THE STATE AND THE FEDERAL SYSTEM: A COMPLEX RELATIONSHIP

Like the other states, California is part of the American federal system. *Federalism* distributes power to both the national and state governments, thereby creating a system of dual citizenship and authority. It is a complex arrangement designed to assure the unity of the country while at the same time permitting the states to reflect the diversity of their people and economies. Although national and state authorities overlap in such areas as taxation and highway construction (examples of so-called concurrent powers), each level of government also has its own policy domain. The U.S. Constitution gives the national government its powers, including such areas as immigration law, interstate commerce, foreign policy, national defense, and international relations. The states are permitted to do anything that is not prohibited or that the Constitution does not assign to the national government. Serious conflicts may occur when states challenge federal laws, such as California's medical marijuana law, which voters approved through initiative (Proposition 215, 1996). The gap between federal drug enforcement and California's more relaxed approach to marijuana use has yet to be resolved.

Within each state, the distribution of powers is *unitary*. This means that the cities, counties, and other units of local government get their authority from the state. States and their local bodies generally focus their powers on such services as education, public safety, and health and welfare.

Just as California has a mighty impact on the country as a whole, the national government exerts influence on the state. Federal funds often come with strings attached. For example, federal highway funds require specific safety laws, including seatbelt regulations, and even *mandate* the age at which individuals may purchase alcohol. In the San Joaquin Valley, California's enormous agricultural center, federal water policies have led to vast croplands going dry, creating "dustbowls" and high unemployment where crops once grew.[3]

In other cases, federal policy fuels the state's economy. For nearly 50 years, between World War II and the end of the Cold War, California's private defense industry relied heavily on federal contracts to create a thriving military-based economy. Major corporations, such as Lockheed, Hughes, and Rockwell, enjoyed high profits and provided well-paying, secure jobs to engineers, managers, secretaries, and assembly-line workers. When the Cold War ended in 1989, this entire military contract system was suddenly downsized and many military bases closed, leaving a huge hole in the California economy. Federal stimulus money under the American Recovery and Reinvestment Act of 2009 held off some of the impacts of the severe recession, but those federal dollars will not continue indefinitely. California continues to seek other sources of economic growth, involving both public and private investment in computer software development, entertainment, tourism, public transportation, and biotechnology, including stem cell research (encouraged by a voter-approved bond measure in 2004).

While relations between the federal government and each state are complex and significant, the relations between states are also important. The U.S. Constitution requires every state to honor the laws of every other state, so that marriages and other contracts made in one state are respected in all states and criminals trying to escape justice cannot find safe haven by leaving the state in which they have been convicted.

Federalism's distribution of powers permits states to enact their diverse policy preferences into law on such matters as gambling, prostitution, trash disposal, and wilderness protection, and thus encourages experiments that

DEBATING THE ISSUES

POPULATION GROWTH: HOW TO FACE THE FUTURE

Viewpoint: We must prepare California for the future by building roads, schools, water systems, and all the infrastructure for the projected future population.

- Immigration rates and birth rates will continue to increase, and the state must be able to provide for the people of the future.
- If we don't prepare now, future Californians will suffer from inadequate housing, heavy traffic, crowded schools, and a reduced quality of life.
- No walls, fences, or immigration agents will be able to keep out people whose alternative is to stay in their country living in poverty.
- People will risk everything for a better life, so we should adapt our laws and infrastructure to accept their presence.
- The labor of immigrants will be needed in the future.

Viewpoint: We must reduce population growth by tightening federal immigration laws and finding a way to keep people from coming to California.

- California cannot sustain the people it has, and cannot absorb more.
- California's congressional delegation and voters must insist on a tighter border using the latest technology to prevent illegal immigration.
- Developed nations cannot continue to absorb the world's poor; we must find ways for less developed nations to advance their own economies so that their people can stay home.

Ask Yourself: How do today's decisions impact the future quality of life in California?

may spread to other states. California has often served as the trial run on new political ideas that later spread to other states. *Conservative* themes such as tax revolts, anti-immigration sentiments, and the backlash against affirmative action all began as successful ballot propositions in California, while *liberal* ideas such as legalization of marijuana for medical purposes and government-provided health care for all also have become ballot battles.

Because federalism allows states great autonomy, and because California has developed a complex web of local governments, the average California voter must make numerous decisions at election time. Each Californian, whether or not a U.S. citizen, lives in a number of election jurisdictions, including a congressional district, a state Senate district, an Assembly district, and a county supervisorial district, plus (in most cases) a city, a school district, and a community college district. (See Figure 1.1

Partisan Offices			
National Level	**Elected by**	**Term**	**Election Year**
President	Entire state	4 years	Years divisible by four
U.S. Senators	Entire state	6 years	Every six years counting from 1992
			Every six years counting from 1994
Members of Congress	Districts	2 years	Even-numbered years
State Level			
Governor[1]			
Lt. Governor[1]			
Secretary of State[1]	Entire state	4 years	Even-numbered years when there is no presidential election
Controller[1]			
Treasurer[1]			
Attorney General[1]			
Insurance Commissioner			
Members of Board of Equalization[1]	Districts	4 years	Same as governor
State Senators[1]	Districts	4 years	Same as governor for even-numbered districts
			Same as president for odd-numbered districts
Assembly members[2]	Districts	2 years	Even-numbered years
Nonpartisan Offices			
State Level			
Superintendent of Public Instruction	Entire state	4 years	Same as governor
Supreme Court justices	Entire state	12 years	Same as governor
Court of Appeal justices	Entire state	12 years	Same as governor
Superior Court judges	Counties	6 years	Even-numbered years

[1]Limited to two terms by Proposition 140
[2]Limited to three terms by Proposition 140

FIGURE 1.1   **Federal and State Officials Elected by California Voters**

Source: League of Women Voters.

for the officials elected by California voters.) This array of political jurisdictions provides many opportunities to exercise democracy. It also creates confusion, overlaps, and many occasions on which voters feel unable to fully evaluate the qualifications of candidates or the merits of ballot propositions.

Other problems linked to federalism include outdated state boundaries that have created some "superstates," with land masses and populations that may be ungovernable, and differences in resources between states. California's large territory could theoretically include two or three states. Meanwhile, variations in states' resources perpetuate inequality in schools, public hospitals, and other government facilities at a time when the nation as a whole is concerned about how to provide these services. The federal system also promotes rivalry between states as they compete to attract new businesses (and jobs) or keep existing ones. Among the tactics used in this struggle are tax breaks, reduced worker compensation, and relaxed environmental protection standards. Even Hollywood, the historic center of the entertainment industry, is suffering from *runaway production*, meaning the decisions to produce films, television shows, and commercials in places where costs are lower. On the larger international scale, thanks to *globalization*, products such as automobiles, clothing, and many other goods are increasingly manufactured abroad, because cheap labor and international treaties combine to create inexpensive products thus reducing domestic job opportunities. California is still a player; but without the long-term planning necessary to promote a productive economy, it remains unclear whether the state can regain some of its former successes.

QUESTIONS TO CONSIDER

Using Your Text and Your Own Experiences

1. What are some of the pros and cons of life in California? Do these depend in part on whether you live in a rural or an urban area?

2. What are some of the challenges facing our state? What can elected officials do to resolve these challenges? How do you fit into the challenges facing our state?

3. Take a class survey. How many students were born in California? How many are immigrants, either from another state or another nation? Team up so that an "immigrant" is paired with a "native" Californian. Teams or pairs can discuss the different experiences of those born here versus those who immigrated.

ENJOYING MEDIA

Movies to See and Web sites to Explore

California State Home Page   ca.gov
Portal to California's Government, Tourism, Economy, etc.

Center for California Studies   csus.edu/calst/index.html
California State University Sacramento's research institute covers politics and more.

Public Policy Institute of California   ppic.org
A nonprofit, nonpartisan independent research institute with a focus on economic issues.

Berkeley in the Sixties, Mark Kitchell, 1990
Documentary depicts Free Speech Movement during the 1960s at UC Berkeley and what happened to the student activists over the next two decades. Some of those student leaders ended up in the state legislature later in life.

El Norte, Gregory Nava, 1983
Guatemalans flee their country's war by going north to California without documents (illegally). Gives a sense of what people are willing to endure in order to get to a better life in California.

ENDNOTES

1. Richard Walker and Ashok Bhardan, "California, Pivot of the Great Recession," UC Berkeley Institute for Research on Labor and Employment, March 2010. http://metrostudies.berkeley.edu/pubs/reports/Walker_93.pdf.
2. *Just the Facts: California's Tax Burden*, Public Policy Institute of California, June 2003.
3. Sonia Verma, "How Green Was My Valley: California's Drought," July 25, 2009. http://www.theglobeandmail.com/news/world/how-green-was-my-valley-californias-drought/article1230646/.

CHAPTER TWO

The Californians: Land, People, and Political Culture

If they can't do it in California, it can't be done anywhere.
—Taylor Caldwell, author

The political process in California, as in other states, is conditioned by many geographic, demographic, and cultural influences. Whereas geography changes only slowly, population shifts and cultural influences can rather suddenly add new and unpredictable threads to the complex web that forms the state's identity and future prospects.

GEOGRAPHIC INFLUENCES: WHERE ARE WE?

With an area of 156,000 square miles, California is larger than Italy, Japan, or England and is the third largest state in the United States, following Alaska and Texas. It is shaped like a gigantic stocking, with a length more than twice its width. If California were superimposed on the East Coast, it would cover six states, from Florida to New York.[1] Despite all the land available, the state's primary urban development has been coastal, with the Bay Area and the Los Angeles Basin as the first areas of growth. More recently, the "Inland Empire" (San Bernardino and Riverside counties) and the San Joaquin Valley have experienced growth, leading to the term "the Third California," although the huge number of home foreclosures and the high unemployment in these areas may ultimately impact growth predictions.[2]

While California's size has contributed to its political dynamics, its location is equally important. As the leading state on what is called the Pacific Rim (those states bordering the Pacific Ocean and facing the Far East), California is the nation's number one exporter. California is also one of only 15 states that border a foreign nation. In part as a result of its proximity to Mexico, Californians of Mexican descent have become the largest ethnic group in the state, one that includes both first-generation Mexican immigrants and "Chicanos," whose parents or ancestors originally came from that country. Nearly half of California's immigrants in recent years have come from Mexico,[3] and as of the 2010 census, California had the largest Hispanic (from all nationalities) population of any state (14 million).[4]

Two other geographic influences command attention: rich natural resources and spectacularly beautiful terrain. Between the majestic Sierra Nevada range along the eastern border and the Coastal Mountains on the west lies the Central Valley—one of the richest agricultural regions in the world. For generations, Central Valley farmers have used water supplies brought from the northern section of the state via the California Aqueduct, making California the nation's leader in farm output, including the underground crop, marijuana (which is often grown on California's "lost coast" in the northwest of the state).[5] However, unpredictable water supplies (after a long drought, the state recently celebrated adequate water, at least for a while) make water distribution a fierce battleground, pitting north versus south, rural versus urban areas, and environmentalists versus farmers.[6] Over 40 percent of the state is forested, and this magnificent resource creates tension between those who want to protect forests and those who want to sustain some form of lumber industry, and, in one particular region, those who want Sonoma wine-grapes grown on those same lands.[7] California has plentiful oil, some of which lies off the 1,000-mile-long coast in locations that have been protected for decades from drilling, although efforts to restart offshore drilling in Santa Barbara were recently renewed and defeated in the state legislature.[8]

Although agriculture, timber, and oil remain economically important as well as environmentally controversial, another natural resource has become the subject of continual political debate over how much to exploit it: California's landscape. Ranging across arid deserts, a 1,000-mile shoreline, and remote mountain wilderness, the terrain itself is a continuing battlefield between conservationists and commercial recreation developers, with the state's need for tourism competing with the preservation approach. Much of California is owned by the public; the state boasts 43 national parks, forests, recreation areas, and monuments, plus its own vast acreage of public lands, including 270 state parks and beaches, some of which are now closed or operated by private vendors due to state budget cuts.[9] Although California includes vast undeveloped lands, Californians are a largely urban people, with over 80 percent living in cities.[10]

DEMOGRAPHIC INFLUENCES: WHO ARE WE?

With rare, short-term exceptions, modern California has a consistent pattern of population growth. Although recent economic slowdowns push more people to leave the state to find work or less expensive places to live, the total number of Californians continues to increase as a result of birth rates (49 percent of population growth), domestic immigration (11 percent), and international immigration (40 percent of total growth).[11] Californians over 65 years old will comprise almost 20 percent of the total population,[12] with vast implications for health care and other services needed by seniors. Long-term predictions suggest that the state will have nearly 47 million people by the year 2025, creating enormous challenges regarding housing, education, health care, transportation, water supplies, and environmental quality. Demographers still predict that California will likely remain the most populous state, with over 12 percent of the nation's people, and with a Latino majority by 2016.[13] All population data are questionable, however, because some people unfortunately refuse to participate in the U.S. Census, and the Census Bureau acknowledges its own struggles to accurately count Californians.[14]

California also continues to be the most diverse state, with residents from virtually every nation and ethnic group on the planet. There is

DEBATING THE ISSUES

ASSIMILATION VS. DIVERSITY

Viewpoint: Immigrants should learn American customs, learn English, and adopt our ways of life quickly and thoroughly.

- Social harmony and basic daily communication suffer when people live in ethnic enclaves and speak only their original language.
- The costs to government and society of offering bilingual education, multilingual election materials, court interpreters, etc., should be eliminated and the money used for other needs.
- People who remain isolated in ethnic communities are more likely to be victims of crime because they lack knowledge of our laws and customs.

Viewpoint: Immigrants should retain their languages, their culture, and customs no matter how long they live in California.

- California's rich culture is enhanced by the huge variety of languages, events, and traditions that exist here.
- People can retain their language and customs and still learn English, becoming multicultural.
- A "monotone" society of one huge blended culture would reduce economic and social options for all.

Ask Yourself: In your community, what is the current balance of diversity and assimilation? How do you feel about it? Why?

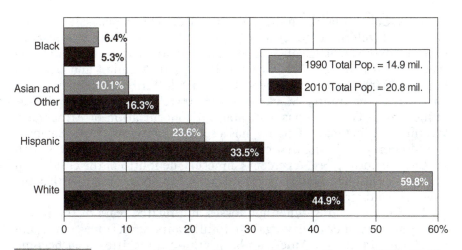

FIGURE 2.1 California Labor Force by Ethnic Group, 1990–2010: Percentage of Labor Force Population
Source: Center for Continuing Study of the California Economy.

no "majority" group, and California has more people who identify themselves as "multiracial" than any other state.[15] (Figure 2.1 breaks down the workforce by ethnic group.) About 25 percent of Californians were born in other nations, with the top three "sending nations" being Mexico, the Philippines, and Vietnam.[16] California has more undocumented immigrants (2.7 million) than any other state, but more recently, the *recession* itself has reduced illegal immigration, as the word gets out that there are fewer jobs for the low-skilled.[17] Ongoing international immigration adds to the state's socioeconomic gaps, since even two-parent working immigrant families are often living at poverty level, giving California the nation's highest poverty rates.[18] Immigrant communities (and even many individual families) are a complex combination of undocumented immigrants, legal residents, political refugees, and foreign-born *naturalized* U.S. citizens. Many immigrants spend years in paperwork as they wait for the federal Bureau of Citizenship and Immigration Services (formerly known as the Immigration and Naturalization Service) to process their applications and move them from refugee status to legal resident, or from resident to citizen status. Both legal and illegal immigrants who are not citizens make up nearly 20 percent of Californians, none of whom can vote, yet all of whom are affected by electoral decisions.[19] During the transition years, *assimilation* takes place to varying degrees, as individuals decide whether to learn English, how much education to seek, and how much to "Americanize" their customs.

Whether they are citizens or residents, concentrations of immigrant ethnic groups have already altered the social and political landscape in many California communities. Out of choice or necessity, ethnic enclaves develop wherever a group puts down roots, their presence reflected in the language of storefront signs, distinctive architecture, and types of food available. Daly City is called "Little Manila," and Fresno is home to 30,000 Hmong, members of a Laotian hill tribe. Sacramento has a large Slavic community; Stockton has 35,000 refugees from several areas of Indochina; Glendale has a substantial concentration of Armenians; Westminster, in Orange County, has a section known as "Little Saigon"; and Monterey Park, the first city in the continental United States with an Asian majority,[20] is 56 percent Chinese. One-fourth of the children in California's public schools are considered "English learners," with some large school districts serving as many as 80 language groups.[21]

During *recessions*, when job losses and related fears of the future create anxiety, negativity against immigrants sometimes rises, and both immigrants and American-born ethnic minorities may become victims of harassment or prejudice. Because people often judge others based on appearance, American-born Latinos and Asians may be subject to prejudices and discrimination based on either ethnic stereotypes or anti-immigrant attitudes. Meanwhile, African Americans, the third largest ethnic minority group, continue to see their numbers decline in proportion to the fast-growing Latino and Asian communities, with resulting concerns about how blacks can compete successfully for educational, economic, and political opportunities while other ethnic groups begin to dominate numerically.

Population diversity, of course, embraces far more than ethnicity. Collectively, Californians seem to embody virtually the whole range of religious beliefs, including 21 percent who belong to no religion. California, being 36 percent Protestant, 31 percent Roman Catholic, 3 percent Jewish, and 9 percent "other," has no "majority religion." Like many Americans, a large number of Californians refer to themselves as "spiritual" rather than religious, and one-third of Californians seldom or never enter a house of worship.[22]

Another of California's diverse groupings is the gay community, whose desire for the right to marry has created enormous political battles, including the continuing political fallout over Proposition 8 (November 2008). Nearly 60 percent of Californians state that "homosexuality should be accepted," yet just over half voted to ban gay marriage. Other issues include the rights of gay or lesbian couples to adopt children, and the general recognition of *Gay, Lesbian, Bisexual, and Transgender (GLBT)* individuals. Gay bashing, a form of violent hostility (and a hate crime), in which an individual is attacked for his or her perceived sexual orientation, brings tragic consequences and outrage. Though still a distinct minority, the seven-member GLBT caucus of the state legislature includes legislators who are openly homosexual and who unite to represent this portion of the population.

CALIFORNIA'S POLITICAL CULTURE: HOW WE THINK

Each state has a distinctive political style that is shaped not only by its geography and population characteristics but also by the values and attitudes shared by most of its people. These elements constitute what is sometimes called the political culture. In a state so diverse, there are multiple worlds, subcultures for everything from religious communities and ethnic groups to organizations bonded by their love of antique cars, native plants, folk dancing, or a myriad of other personal interests. Increasingly, these divergent groups do not share any political or social framework from which to make coherent public policy choices.

In terms of socioeconomic differences, California is more of a *two-tier* state than some others. In fact, California is multitiered, with huge gaps between those at the top and those at the bottom of the income levels. During both economic growth periods and declines, the major cause of vast inequalities in household incomes is the increasing gap between private corporate salaries and the low-wage working poor. The incomes of the wealthiest 5 percent of families increased by 50 percent between the late 1970s and late 1990s, while the poorest fifth of the state's families lost 5 percent of their income during the same period.[23] Middle-income families have been seriously damaged by the current recession, with home foreclosures, layoffs, and bankruptcies creating downward mobility for thousands of Californians.

Unlike the highest income earners, Californians of modest or low incomes are challenged by the high cost of housing,[24] inadequate health care for the one-fifth of Californians who are uninsured, and the increasing cost of public higher education opportunities. Decisions made by Sacramento have led to enormous increases in the cost of tuition at the University of California, California State University, and public community colleges (Figure 2.2), while public health-care options have also been severely reduced by the state. Policy experts warn that if California cannot educate its future workforce adequately, the state's economic strengths will be seriously undermined.[25]

With all the economic and social difficulties they face, it's no surprise that Californians may use their votes to show serious frustration with their political leaders. In 2003, voters used the *recall* process to remove Governor Gray Davis and replace him with Arnold Schwarzenegger. Then in both 2005 and 2009, voters defeated an array of ballot measures promoted by Governor Schwarzenegger as his solutions for the state. California's *electorate* continues to be mostly white, older, and more affluent, even though the population of the state is diverse, young, and of moderate or low income. Even with a large push for "vote by mail," in which people vote by mailing in their ballots before election day, and with some counties experimenting with

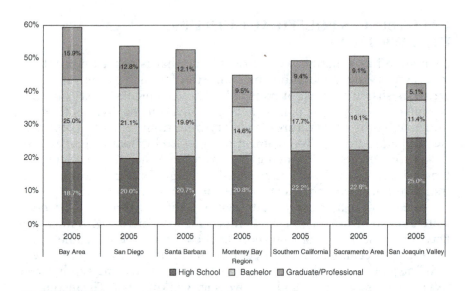

FIGURE 2.2 **Educational Attainment**

Source: Share of Population by Highest Level of Education 2005.

touch-screen voting, potential voters too often ignore their opportunity to determine electoral outcomes.

Although not all eligible citizens bother to vote, the recognition of government's power motivates many Californians to form political associations to represent their views. Because of the ethnic, socioeconomic, and cultural diversity of the state, California is home to a wide variety of political organizations. The ideologies behind many of the organizations can be simplistically summarized by the traditional labels of American politics: *conservative* and *liberal.* The *conservative* side of California politics is torn between those who support maximum freedom for both business and individuals and those who like free enterprise but prefer government to regulate personal behavior such as sexuality and abortion. These uneasy partners form the basis of the California Republican Party, and their areas of agreement are primarily linked to limiting taxes and decreasing government activities through *privatization.* Moderate Republicans, especially women, often feel conflicted between their beliefs in smaller government and lower taxes and their desire for the right to abortion. Republicans running for governor may win a primary by being a strict conservative, but in the general election, Republicans rarely win unless they are pro-choice and pro-gay rights.

On the other side of the political spectrum, the *liberal* movement in California has deep roots, holding firm to a belief in the value of government as a mechanism to improve people's lives. Liberals generally advocate positions which favor a woman's right to control her reproductive future; full gay rights, including gay marriage; and support

COMPARED TO CALIFORNIA

SAME-SEX MARRIAGE LAWS

California: For a brief period in 2004, gay marriage was legal in San Francisco, and about 18,000 couples were married. In 2008, voters narrowly passed Proposition 8, which denies homosexual couples the right to marry. The constitutionality of Proposition 8 is still being determined by the federal courts; meanwhile, those married during the brief period that gay marriage was legal are considered married by the state of California.

New York, Massachusetts, Connecticut, New Hampshire, Iowa, and Vermont: Same-sex couples may marry under current law.

Canada: Same-sex marriage has been legal in Canada since 2005.

Think Critically: Why do some people compare same-sex marriage to interracial marriage? What is the history of miscegenation law? Find out which states have passed gay marriage rights into law.

for labor unions and universal health care. Being too liberal is probably just as bad for a California politician as being too conservative; the voters statewide trend toward the middle. But political labels are only one aspect of California's complex polity: Many Californians are uninterested in traditional political labels and, in the noble American pragmatic tradition, just want to solve problems. At the moment, the Golden State has plenty of problems to face and resolve.

QUESTIONS TO CONSIDER

Using Your Text and Your Own Experiences

1. What is the relationship between California's geography (size, location, topography, etc.) and its economic and political situation?
2. What are some of the pros and cons of the state's ethnic diversity?
3. Discuss the issue of social and economic inequality. What problems are caused by the vast gaps between rich and poor? Are there any advantages to having a two-tier society?

ENJOYING MEDIA

Movies to See and Web sites to Explore

U.S. Census Data   census.gov
Massive amounts of statistics about demographics, population, and trends in society.

Border Region Information   borderecoweb.sdsu.edu
California is one of the states that borders Mexico, with many implications
for the state's economy and social issues.

California Research Bureau   library.ca.gov
Data about California history, genealogy, public policy, and more.

Sideways, Alexander Payne, 2004
Two friends take a trip through California's southern wine country, the
Santa Ynez Valley, and interact with a variety of people. The film gives
a taste of the ethnic diversity of California and the natural beauty of the
Santa Barbara area.

Crash, Paul Haggis, 2004
Traffic collisions and ethnic clashes express some truths about Los
Angeles in this Oscar-winning film. The film leaves you wondering if we
can ever learn to get along.

ENDNOTES

1. *Los Angeles Times*, December 17, 1987, Part 1, p. 3.
2. Joel Kotkin and William Frey, "The Third California," *Los Angeles Times*, January 29, 2006, p. M1.
3. Laura E. Hill and Joseph M. Hayes, "California's Newest Immigrants," *California Counts*, Public Policy Institute of California, Vol. 5, No. 2, November 2003, p. 1.
4. "United States Bureau of the Census," *California Quick Facts*, 2010. http:// quickfacts.census.gov/qfd/states/06000.html.
5. Jon Gettman, "Marijuana Production in the United States," 2006. http:// www.drugscience.org/Archive/bcr2/domstprod.html.
6. Ellen Hanak and Jay Lund, "Adapting California's Water Management to Climate Change," Public Policy Institute of California, November 2008.
7. Louis Sahagun and P. J. Huffstutter, "A Tale of Grape vs. Redwood," *Los Angeles Times*, August 25, 2011, p. A1.
8. John Mann, "Assembly Votes Down Governor's Offshore Oil Drilling Proposal," *Santa Barbara Noozhawk.com*, July 24, 2009. http://www. noozhawk.com/local_news/article/072409_assembly_votes_down_governors_ offshore_drilling_proposal/.
9. "Park Closure List," California State Park Web site, July 2011. http://www. parks.ca.gov/?page_id=26685.
10. "81% of Californians Live in Cities, State Agency Says," *Los Angeles Times*, May 5, 1999, p. A38.
11. California Department of Finance, *Population Growth by Types of Sources, 2000–2004*, cited in Southern California Association of Governments, The State of the Region 2005, December 2005.
12. Hans P. Johnson, *California Population*, Public Policy Institute of California, July 2009.
13. Ibid. http://www.ppic.org/content/pubs/report/R_709HJR.pdf.

14. Robin Fields, "State Census Sampling Shows Huge Undercount," *Los Angeles Times*, December 7, 2002, p. B10.
15. Solomon Moore, "State Leads Nation in Mixed-Race Individuals," *Los Angeles Times*, November 29, 2001, p. B8.
16. Hill and Hayes, "California's Newest Immigrants," p. 3.
17. Teresa Watanabe, "Illegal Immigration Slows in California," *Los Angeles Times*, April 15, 2009, p. A21.
18. Mary C. Daly, Deborah Reed, and Heather N. Royer, "Population Mobility and Income Inequality in California," *California Counts*, Public Policy Institute of California, Vol. 2, No. 4, May 2001, p. 1.
19. Joaquin Avila, "Political Apartheid in California: Consequences of Excluding a Growing Noncitizen Population," *Latino Policy and Issues Brief*, No. 9 (Los Angeles: UCLA Chicano Studies Research Center, December 2003), p. 1.
20. Seth Mydans, "Asian Investors Create a Pocket of Prosperity," *New York Times*, October 17, 1994, p. A8.
21. Sonya M. Tafoya, "The Linguistic Landscape of California Schools," *California Counts*, Public Policy Institute of California, Vol. 3, No. 4, February 2002, p. 1.
22. "The Pew Forum on Religion and Public Life," Religious Composition of California, 2008. http://www.pewforum.org/religion08/state.php?StateID=1.
23. David Carroll and Jean Ross, *Boom, Bust and Beyond: The State of Working California* (Sacramento, CA: California Budget Project, 2003).
24. Steven F. Hayward, "Preserving the American Dream: The Facts about Suburban Communities and Housing Choice," California Building Industry Association/Building Industry Institute, September 1996.
25. Hans Johnson, "Educating California: Choices for the Future," *California 2025* (San Francisco: Public Policy Institute of California, 2009).

CHAPTER THREE

California's Historical Development

The roads that lead to California are long roads.
They are journeys, migrations, exiles.
— Mark Arax, journalist

California's modern history begins with the native population of about 300,000 people in approximately 100 linguistic/cultural "tribelets," who lived on this land before the Europeans arrived.[1] Despite the unique culture of each of the dozens of Native California tribes, very little information exists regarding the diverse groups that inhabited California during this period. Perhaps that is because these first Californians were nearly exterminated. According to a New York newspaper in 1860, "in [other] States, the Indians have suffered wrongs and cruelties.... But history has no parallel to the recent atrocities perpetrated in California. Even the record of Spanish butcheries in Mexico and Peru has nothing so diabolical."[2] The hunter-gatherers of California were soon annihilated to make room for the *conquistadores*, whose desire for gold led them to murder and rape many of the people they found here.[3]

THE SPANISH ERA: 1542–1822

In 1542, only 50 years after Columbus first came to the "New" World, Spain claimed California as a result of a voyage by Juan Rodriguez Cabrillo. More than two centuries passed, however, before the Spanish established their first colony. It was named San Diego and was founded by an expedition headed by Gaspar de Portola, a military commander, and Junipero Serra, a missionary dedicated to converting the Indians to Roman Catholicism. Between 1769 and 1823, the Spanish conquerors built 22 missions from San Diego to Sonoma, each with its own military post. By the time the missions were completed, most of the Native Californians had been destroyed by overwork, disease, and brutality. Meanwhile, farther south, the *mestizo* residents of New Spain (primarily what is now Mexico, Central America, and many of the Spanish-speaking South American colonies) were ready to overthrow the Spanish colonial rulers and declare independence.

MEXICAN DOMINANCE: 1821–1848

In 1821, Mexico won independence from Spain. Soon after, the land now called California (as well as the modern states of Utah, Colorado, New Mexico, and Arizona) officially became part of the new United States of Mexico. Civilian governments were established for the pueblos, or villages, but the distant government in Mexico City still viewed California as a remote and relatively unimportant colony.

American settlers began to arrive in the 1840s, lured by the inviting climate and stories of economic opportunities. Many were filled with the spirit of *manifest destiny*, a belief that Americans had a mission to control the whole continent. When the United States failed in its attempt to buy California, it used a Texas boundary dispute as an excuse to launch war with Mexico in 1846. The United States declared victory within a year, thus winning the right to purchase at bargain rates enormous lands including California, Arizona, New Mexico, and Texas, as well as large parts of Utah, Colorado, and Nevada. California came under American military rule, and in 1848 Mexico renounced its claims by signing the Treaty of Guadalupe Hidalgo, a document that promised the Mexican population of California that their language and property would be respected under the new government—a promise that was quickly broken. Within a short time, the ranchos of the *Californios* (people of Mexican descent) were grabbed by immigrants (mostly Anglos), and much of these lands were later granted to the owners of the railroads.[4]

AMERICANIZATION AND STATEHOOD: 1848–1850

The U.S. military occupation lasted three years while Congress battled over how to manage its vast new territories. The turning point was the discovery of gold in 1848, encouraging "Forty-niners" from all over the world to head to California. By 1849, the population quadrupled, and the settlers adopted the first California constitution. Meanwhile, the U.S. Congress postponed the Civil War through enacting the Compromise of 1850 (which kept a balance of slave and free states) by admitting California as a free state. California became the thirty-first state and the first that did not border an existing state. (Figure 3.1 shows the county boundaries of California today.)

FIGURE 3.1 **Map of California**
Source: Los Angeles County Almanac, 1991.

Today the legacy of the Spanish and Mexican periods can be found in California's population itself, as well as in the missions, architecture, and city names. History does not easily erase itself; California's Spanish/Mexican roots pervade the culture.

CONSOLIDATING POWER: 1850–1902

During its first 50 years of statehood, California grew in both population and diversity. Newcomers from around the world came to seek their fortunes, and some were extraordinarily successful. Others, particularly during economic downturns, began to *scapegoat* less popular groups and call for their expulsion. Chinese immigrants, brought to this country to build the railroads cheaply, were major targets of overt racism and discrimination during the recession of the 1870s. Despite occasional downturns, the overall economy boomed during the 1880s and 1890s, although the *Californios* generally became impoverished and forgotten as white Americans took charge. The economy shifted from mining to agriculture, and the arrival of the transcontinental railroad brought people from across the nation eager to begin new lives and find a share of California's richness.

In 1879, the first state constitution was replaced by the one now in effect. In a preview of political events that seem to recur every time the state's economy sags, the second California constitution was loaded with anti-immigrant provisions (aimed at Asian immigrants), which were later declared invalid as violations of the U.S. Constitution.

THE PROGRESSIVE LEGACY: 1902–1919

The *Progressive movement* in California, led by Hiram Johnson, arose at the beginning of the twentieth century. Its goal was to reduce the power of corrupt political parties and rich corporations that spent large sums to control politicians. In California, the primary target was the Southern Pacific Railroad, a corporation that owned one-fifth of all nonpublic land in the state. Its major stockholders—Charles Crocker, Leland Stanford, Collis P. Huntington, and Mark Hopkins—were the "Big Four" of state politics. According to their critics, they had bought "the best state legislature that money could buy."

Despite the power of the Big Four, the Progressives had remarkable success. Child labor laws and conservation policies were adopted. Political parties were weakened by imposing rigid legal controls on their internal organization and prohibiting candidates for city, county, and judicial offices and education boards from mentioning their party affiliation on the ballot. Today, all of these offices remain *nonpartisan*, with only names and occupations listed on the ballot.

Possibly the most important legacies left by the Progressives were the *direct democracy* powers that permit voters to pass laws or amend the state constitution through the ballot box, as well as to recall elected officials from office through a special election. The Progressive reforms of 1911 also brought suffrage to California women, nine years before they won the right to vote in federal elections.

CHANGING THE CONSTITUTION

California: Amendments to the state constitution require a majority vote in a statewide election. A proposal for a State Constitutional Convention also requires voter approval.

United States: There are several variations, but U.S. history shows that virtually all amendments to the U.S. Constitution have met the following requirements: a two-third vote of Congress, plus ratification by three-fourths of the state legislatures. (There is no popular vote required.)

Think Critically: Should it be easy or hard to change the basic document of a state or nation? Why do Californians amend their state constitution so frequently?

THE TWENTIETH CENTURY, CALIFORNIA STYLE

In the last century, California experienced many of the same major events as the rest of the nation did: the Roaring Twenties, the Great Depression, and the World War II economic boom. California's contributions to American history of these periods include the near election of a socialist governor in 1934 (and the *redbaiting* campaign to defeat him), the Depression-era migration of hundreds of thousands of people from the Midwest Dust Bowl to the Golden State, and the *repatriation* of 600,000 U.S. citizens of Mexican descent who were deported from California as official scapegoats for the economic woes of the era.[5] During World War II, Japanese Californians were deported to detention "camps," and their homes and businesses were confiscated as they became the target of wartime scapegoating. When the economy boomed during the Cold War, new arrivals were once again welcomed to help develop the aerospace/defense industries. Throughout the century, through good and bad times, California's population continued to grow.

The long period of relative prosperity during the 1950s and 1960s did not touch everyone. When cheap labor was needed in the agricultural fields during World War II, for example, Mexican *braceros* entered the country with temporary work permits but were expelled when their labor was no longer needed.[6] People of color experienced discrimination in housing, employment, and education. By the early 1960s, California's educational system was rocked by the street protests of UC Berkeley students protesting their own lack of free speech on campus as well as the unequal treatment of blacks in Bay Area businesses.[7] By the end of the 1960s, California was known as the center of a counterculture of drugs, antiwar sentiment, and sexual experimentation in places like San Francisco's Haight-Ashbury neighborhood.

The 1960s, under Governor Pat Brown, also saw immense investment in California's *infrastructure*, and the enactment of the Master Plan for Higher Education, which guaranteed a free community college opportunity and two low-cost public university options for all Californians. Nearly 50 years later, many educators believe that the Master Plan has been nearly destroyed by the fee increases at all three levels of public higher education.

During the *inflationary* period of the 1970s, Californians, enraged by the rapid increases in prices of everything from gasoline to property taxes, voted their frustration by supporting the deep property tax cuts of Proposition 13 (1978). By the 1980s, former California governor Ronald Reagan was president of the United States and the economy again boomed, although the promised "trickle-down" of economic improvements to the poor did not occur. In recent years, a lengthy recession has left 12 percent of Californians unemployed, with resulting loss of tax revenue and severe budget cuts in both state and local agencies.

CALIFORNIA'S CONSTITUTION: A FEW HIGHLIGHTS

Like the national government, the California political system is characterized by a separation of powers, freedom, and democracy. Certain differences, however, deserve attention. Although the separation of powers involves the traditional three branches—legislative, executive, and judicial—each is marked by distinctive state characteristics. For example, the California legislature shares lawmaking authority with the people through the *initiative* process; the governor's power is diminished by the popular election of seven other executive officials; and California judges must be approved by voters. The federal system has none of the *direct democracy* features, nor do federal judges ever appear on the ballot.

Many of the freedoms guaranteed in the state constitution are identical to those protected by the U.S. Constitution. However, the state constitution includes additional rights for its residents. For example, Article I, Section 1, of the California constitution proclaims that "All people are by nature free and independent and have inalienable rights. Among these are enjoying and defending life and liberty, acquiring, possessing, and protecting property, and pursuing and obtaining safety, happiness, and privacy." Similar references to property acquisition, safety, and privacy do not exist in the U.S. Constitution.

California's constitution is much easier to amend than the federal Constitution, and it has been amended (and thus lengthened) over 500 times since 1879. The process involves two steps. First, amendments may be proposed either by a two-thirds vote in both houses of the legislature or by an *initiative* petition signed by 8 percent of the number of voters who voted in the last election for governor. Second, the proposed amendment must appear as a *proposition* on the ballot and must be

---

DEBATING THE ISSUES

CONSTITUTIONAL CHANGE: CALIFORNIA VS. THE UNITED STATES

Viewpoint: The U.S. Constitution is better because it requires enormous social and political agreement in order to be amended.

- A document that defines the governing structure of a society should be difficult to change.
- Super-majorities are important in making major changes to ensure real social agreement.

Viewpoint: The California constitution is better because it is easily amended by a vote of the people.

- Change occurs rapidly and should be easily adapted into constitutions.
- California's direct democracy provides power to the public as the most important voice in changing how our government operates.

Ask Yourself: Do most people know how constitutional change works? Should they? Explain your conclusion.

---

approved by a simple majority of voters. As a result of the options created by the Progressives, voters can amend the state constitution without any legislative action.

Having a long, complicated state constitution is not the most efficient way to operate a state. Among the many suggestions for future constitutional revisions (via ballot initiatives) are to alter term limits to allow experienced legislators to stay longer, to allow local governments more options to impose taxes, to amend Proposition 13 so that corporate property can be taxed at current values, and to change the actual structure of California's direct democracy.

QUESTIONS TO CONSIDER

Using Your Text and Your Own Experiences

1. Who were the first Californians? Why and how were they almost totally destroyed by those who came next?

2. What is the most important contribution of the Progressive movement in California? How would the Progressives feel about contemporary California politics?

3. What are some ways that California's history impacts life today, including culture, politics, ethnic diversity, and immigration?

ENJOYING MEDIA

Movies to See and Web sites to Explore

Californiality   Californiality.com
Blogging on culture, politics, government, and people of California.

California Historical Society   calhist.org
The online guide to over 300 years of California history.

California Geographical Survey   geogdata.csun.edu
Portal to maps of California and surrounding states.

The Mask of Zorro, 1998
A highly fictional action adventure about California's early days and its struggle to free itself from Spanish colonial rule, aided by the masked crusader. Raises the issues of mythology vs. reality in California's history.

The Grapes of Wrath, Jon Ford, 1940
The movie adaptation of John Steinbeck's classic tale of a Midwest family which comes to California during the Great Depression seeking a fresh start. Another illustration of the extraordinary pull of California.

Come See the Paradise, Alan Parker, 1991
A white labor organizer falls in love with a Japanese American girl in Los Angeles as World War II begins and she is sent to an internment camp. A film that helps us understand the personal impacts of the political panic that created the Japanese internment.

ENDNOTES

1. Sucheng Chan and Spencer C. Olin, *Major Problems in California History* (New York: Houghton Mifflin, 1997), p. 30.
2. Cited by Alexander Cockburn, "Beat the Devil," *The Nation*, June 24, 1991, p. 839.
3. Antonia I. Castaneda, "Spanish Violence Against Amerindian Women," in Adela de la Torre and Beatriz Pasquera, eds., *Building with Our Hands: New Directions in Chicano Studies* (Berkeley: University of California Press, 1993).
4. "Conflicts Over Land in a New State, 1850s–1870s," in Chan and Olin, eds., *Major Problems in California History*, pp. 110–135.
5. Gregg Jones, "Reparations Sought for '30s Expulsion Program," *Los Angeles Times*, July 16, 2003, p. B8.
6. Stephanie S. Pincetl, *Transforming California: A Political History of Land Use and Development* (Baltimore MD: Johns Hopkins University Press, 1999), p. 174.
7. W. J. Rorabaugh, "Berkeley in the 1960s," in Chan and Olin, eds., *Major Problems in California History*, pp. 375–384.

CHAPTER FOUR

Freedom and Equality: California's Delicate Balance

California is not so much poor as it is unequal.
—Robert Enoch Buck, sociologist

People in California, as everywhere else in a capitalist democracy, must continually reassess choices regarding individual freedom and social justice. *Civil liberties*, such as freedoms of speech, press, and association (which restrict government powers), may conflict with *civil rights*, which often require government protections. California's appellate courts have often been asked to rule on the rights of individuals vs. the rights of the community. Should homeless people be allowed to sleep on public streets, or does their presence create a risk for the community? In Santa Barbara and Laguna Beach, the American Civil Liberties Union has filed cases challenging those cities' antisleeping ordinances, resulting in Laguna Beach revoking its policy.[1] Should high school students be permitted to wear T-shirts with "offensive" language? And is it okay for a sixth-grade girl to do a class presentation about Harvey Milk, the gay San Francisco Supervisor who was assassinated in 1978? All of these issues have resulted in court decisions; in the case of the sixth grader, after the court acted, she received an apology from the school district for its violation of her freedom of speech.[2]

FREEDOM AND SOCIAL RESPONSIBILITY: JUGGLING BETWEEN EXTREMES

In numerous areas where individual freedom (or corporate profits) may conflict with public needs, California's policies have moved from supporting maximum personal freedom to placing some limits on that freedom in order to maximize the well-being of the larger society. Antismoking laws, helmet laws for motorcyclists and children on bicycles, and strict regulations for teen drivers all indicate the state's interest in protecting individuals from each other. In the area of personal privacy (often violated by telemarketers and other businesses), the legislature has struggled to create privacy protections as well to protect Californians from cyber-stalking and identity fraud.[3] In the arena of environmental quality, the traditional struggle between public well-being and business profitability fluctuates between cooperative approaches and outright political battles. A cooperative effort between environmentalists and major industries led to the San Joaquin Valley Air Pollution Control District's research regarding sources of smog in the Central Valley, with an understanding that all sides would benefit from better air quality.[4] In a less collaborative situation, the Los Angeles Regional Water Quality Control Board denied the business community's appeals about high costs and demanded that all new building developments include plans to collect or filter rainwater so that polluted rainwater would not end up in local beaches.[5]

DEBATING THE ISSUES

FREEDOM VS. LICENSE

Viewpoint: Individuals should be allowed to live their lives with minimal government interference.

- The individual is the most important social actor and should have maximum power over his or her life.
- Government should not be a parent or "nanny" protecting people from their own freedom to choose.
- Laws that require people to wear helmets, use seatbelts, or drive without using a cell phone are all forms of government intrusion in private choices.

Viewpoint: Government should make laws to protect people, including protections they prefer not to have.

- People who don't adequately protect themselves (wearing helmets, seatbelts) may be injured and cost everyone tax dollars for their medical care.
- People don't have the right to hurt themselves and possibly others.
- Government must create laws that protect the public as a whole, even if those laws appear as limitations for individuals.

Ask Yourself: Which laws do you consider appropriate government involvement in personal life? Which laws are intrusive and need changing?

In another arena of personal rights, California courts have ruled that individual freedom includes the right *not* to hear a prayer at a public school graduation ceremony. In deference to the vast diversity of religious beliefs among Californians, the state Supreme Court determined that such prayers and invocations are an establishment of religion in violation of the separation of church and state. Despite this ruling, many public schools still offer prayers at football games, graduations, and other tax-sponsored events.

EQUALITY: A CONTINUING CHALLENGE

California's large gaps between wealth and poverty inevitably create vast inequality among individuals. Compounding this socioeconomic inequality, Californians have also been forced to confront a long history of inequality based on racial bigotry. Prejudicial attitudes and discriminatory behaviors are older than the state itself. Only 10 percent of the Native Californians survived the Spanish era, and the first governor after statehood called for the extermination of those who remained. When the United States defeated Mexico in 1848, California Mexicans were gradually marginalized, losing much of the political and economic power they once wielded. Soon after, in the period of economic stagnation of the 1870s, the Chinese immigrants who helped build the transcontinental railroads during the 1860s became the targets of serious forms of racism, including lynchings and the "Chinese exclusion" provision of the 1879 state constitution (which attempted to prohibit Chinese from holding many kinds of jobs). The first official apology from the State Legislature to California's Chinese American community came in 2009.[6]

In today's multicultural California, the issues of equity are more complex than ever. (See Figure 4.1 for California's major population

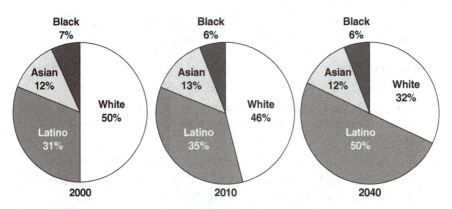

FIGURE 4.1 **Projected Ethnic Breakdown of California's Population**
Source: California Department of Finance, 1998.

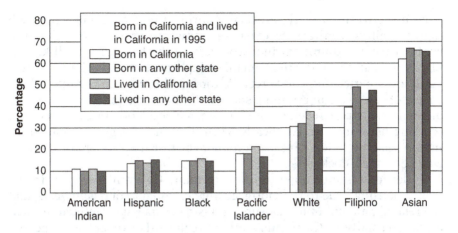

FIGURE 4.2 **Bachelor's Degree Completion in California and the Rest of the United States, by Race, Ethnicity, and Nativity, Ages 25–29, 2000**

Source: Public Policy Institute of California.

groups.) Although Proposition 209 ended all forms of *affirmative action* in public education and state systems, California is far from the "color-blind" utopia to which opponents of affirmative action aspire. Wage gaps clearly divide whites and Asians from African Americans and Latinos, with whites and Asians generally earning more than African Americans and Latinos, primarily owing to the lower educational attainments of the latter two ethnic groups. (See Figure 4.2.) A vicious cycle in which lack of educational opportunities leads to continuing underemployment can extend from generation to generation.

Perhaps it is the underlying economic as well as the educational gaps that add to racial and ethnic tensions. These prejudices exist not only between whites and various minorities, but among minority groups themselves. In urban school districts, high schools may be home to competing ethnic gangs whose rivalry erupts in periodic violence between some combination of Latinos, African Americans, Asians, or Middle Eastern ethnic groups. Inside California's vast prison system, inmates of different ethnic groups were segregated to avoid racial violence until the U.S. Supreme Court declared this racial separation unconstitutional in 2005.

The conflicts among many of California's ethnic groups reflect in part the continuing difficulties created by competition for scarce opportunities. When Governor Brown signed the California DREAM Act (2011), which allows undocumented students with strong academic records to access private scholarships for college, protests came from groups who believe that giving such help to the undocumented will shortchange citizens.

And in the world of work, especially during a recession and a tight job market, subtle limitations exist for nonwhite groups. In the highly competitive entertainment industry, despite the handful of well-known blacks and Latinos in the field, membership statistics for both the Writers Guild of America and the Screen Actors Guild indicate the difficulties people of color face in attaining stardom (or even regular work). In a very different industry, a federal judge has ordered both corporate shippers and the longshore union to pay nearly $3 million in damages to hundreds of minorities who failed a biased employment test used to determine who could become a dockworker.[7]

Additional scarce opportunities for many Californians occur in the area of housing. Due to the mortgage finance collapse of recent years, and the related tsunami of foreclosures, housing costs have declined in most areas, especially in California's inland regions. However, fewer people are eligible to get loans to purchase a home, so the California dream of home ownership remains elusive (Figure 4.3). There does not appear to be any signs of a recovery in the housing market, and some demographers believe that the increase in senior citizens and decline in younger families will leave home sales in decline until perhaps 2020.[8]

Housing may also determine educational opportunities, because public school quality varies in different neighborhoods. Education is the key to a lifetime of increased economic opportunity. The combination of underfunded schools, overcrowding in urban areas, and *white flight* leaves many public school systems with 90 percent nonwhite students, of whom large numbers may need English-language instruction as well

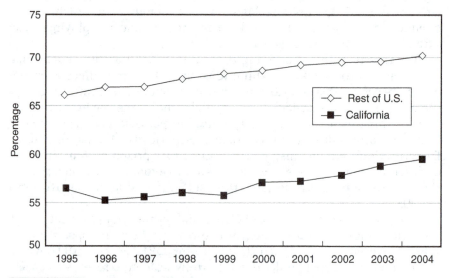

FIGURE 4.3 **Homeownership Rates, 1995–2004**

Source: Public Policy Institute of California.

as all the core courses. While the middle class and wealthy may afford private schools, low-income families must utilize local schools or find time and resources to seek magnet or *charter school* options for their children. The Los Angeles area has the highest number of charter schools (public schools that are exempt from many state and local regulations and are supposedly more creative) in the nation, but success rates for these schools vary enormously. Test scores, graduation rates, college admission data, and other indicators of educational success are almost always lower at underfunded public schools, which are attended predominantly by Latinos and African Americans (typically from low-income families). Figure 4.2 shows Bachelor's Degree completion rates.

Even if California's youth have the qualifications to enter universities, or the motivation to attend a public two-year college (where there are no academic admission requirements), huge fee increases at the two public university systems as well as the community colleges make it harder for low-income Californians to achieve higher education. Financial aid is available, but many eligible Californians do not know how to access financial aid services.

DIVERSITY IN REPRESENTATION: IDENTITY POLITICS IN ACTION

In a continuing American tradition, when ethnic and immigrant communities grow larger, they begin to fight for their share of political and economic power. California's growing ethnic communities have already shifted the demographic pattern: there is no longer any one majority group. By the year 2021, it is predicted that whites will make up about one-third of the population and thus will be a "minority" group, while Latinos, Asians, and blacks together will make up 60 percent (40 percent, 14 percent, and 6 percent, respectively).[9] However, this *demographic shift* does not automatically create an equally rapid shift in political power. Gains for underrepresented groups depend on much more than their population count. Factors that influence access to political power include their rates of voter registration and turnout, their financial ability to support candidates, and their interest in the political process. However, at current levels of voter participation and citizenship among foreign-born immigrants, it is expected that by 2040, whites will represent only 35 percent of voting-age adults but will still be 53 percent of the electorate.[10]

In addition to the issues of citizenship and participation in voting, another factor in political success is the use of financial resources to support candidates and influence elections. Because average household income is lower in many ethnic communities, they do not have the disposable income to support or recruit their own candidates. Coalitions of ethnic groups, including whites, have emerged as a way

COMPARED TO CALIFORNIA

FOREIGN IMMIGRANTS, PERCENTAGE OF TOTAL POPULATION (NOT INCLUDING UNDOCUMENTED IMMIGRANTS)

California: 28 percent

New York: 20 percent

Florida: 18 percent

Texas: 15 percent

Source: Steven A. Camarota, Immigrants at Mid-Decade, Center for Immigration Studies, December 2005, http://www.cis.org/articles/2005/back1405.html

Think Critically: How is California impacted by having over one-fourth of its people born in other nations? What are the positive and negative outcomes?

to promote qualified candidates from a variety of ethnic groups. In keeping with their rapidly increasing population numbers, the number of Latino and Asian American elected officials has grown, and in some communities, city council and school board members increasingly include immigrant politicians eager to be involved in their new country as elected leaders.[11]

One interethnic issue facing the growing number of politically active Latinos (and Asians to a lesser degree) is the high numbers of Latinos moving into formerly African American neighborhoods. Formerly black communities now often are numerically dominated by Latinos, particularly immigrant Latinos. Census data suggest that African Americans (like whites) will continue to decline numerically in proportion to the much faster-growing Latino and Asian groups; African American leaders are therefore concerned about maintaining adequate electoral representation in places like South Los Angeles and Oakland. Some black politicians have made it a point to learn Spanish as a way to improve their connections with their Latino constituents.

Providing better political representation to Latinos through language acquisition is relatively simple because most Latinos have Spanish-language origins, although they may represent 18 different nationalities. In contrast, Asian Americans represent over 30 distinct national and language origins, with the largest populations being Filipino, Chinese, Korean, and Vietnamese. Because the diversity is so enormous, there will never be precise and proportional representation for every ethnic group. Therefore, elected officials, regardless of their own background, must learn to represent everyone and not appeal to narrow ethnic concerns.

In addition to the largest ethnic and racial groups, small but active minority communities are working toward gaining a greater share of political power. Armenian Californians have seen a governor from their heritage elected, while California's growing Islamic population seeks better access to the political process, especially since negative stereotyping and hate crimes have created real fears among some Muslim communities. Native Californians, who compose over 120 tribal groups, have focused their political attention and substantial campaign contributions on issues relating to economic development on tribal land (with a heavy emphasis on building casinos) and protection of their culture. With the state's social diversity likely to continue, political leadership in the twenty-first century will be a rainbow of cultures, all of which might retain their unique identities while also working to represent all Californians.

SEXUAL POLITICS: SLOW CHANGE FOR THE UNDERREPRESENTED

Women have made slow progress since the Women's Liberation movement of the 1960s raised concerns about women's equality and access to power. Although women account for 51 percent of the population, they are nowhere near holding half of the legislative seats, executive positions, judgeships, or local posts available. In one unusual exception, the state Supreme Court now has four (out of seven) women. However, the number of women in the state legislature has dropped since a peak in the 1990s, and many cities have all-male or nearly all-male city councils. Meanwhile, at the nonelected level, thousands of women who are state employees in agencies ranging from the Department of Motor Vehicles to the Employment Development Department earn only about three-fourths as much as men doing the same jobs.[12] In one unfortunate measure of *parity*, the number of women has increased in the state prison system, almost doubling since 1990.[13]

California was the first state to elect two women to the U.S. Senate, Barbara Boxer and Dianne Feinstein, and the home of the first woman Speaker of the House, Nancy Pelosi (D, San Francisco). They are joined in Washington, D.C., by 18 other women in the House of Representatives. Since there are currently no term limits for federal officials, the women in Congress may remain in office for many years. The only challenge for most of them (and for all their male colleagues) is to get reelected from a newly designed district developed under the Citizens Redistricting Commission which was created by the Voters First Act (Proposition 11-2008).

One often invisible and certainly underrepresented minority group (made up of individuals of all ethnicities) is the gay and lesbian community. At one time, openly gay politicians were rare outside of San Francisco or West Hollywood, both magnets for the homosexual population.

Now the state legislature has seven men and women in its *Gay, Lesbian, Bisexual, and Transgender (GLBT)* caucus, including Assembly Speaker John Perez, and numerous local governments have gay and lesbian elected officials. As more gays come *out of the closet* and become politically active, their clout will no doubt increase. However, the gay community has *partisan* differences, with gay Republicans fighting hard for respect in their party and gay Democrats emphasizing the supportiveness of their party's policies.

California's record of electing politicians with diverse backgrounds is certainly better than that of many other states. But perhaps it is inevitable that California will take the lead, since the demographic pattern of increasing diversity is unlikely to change, and trends suggest that the nation will gradually become more like California.

QUESTIONS TO CONSIDER

Using Your Text and Your Own Experiences

1. Discuss some areas where individual freedom (or free enterprise) may conflict with social needs. What is your position on these issues?
2. In what arenas are ethnic minorities underrepresented? Why do these patterns persist even though California has no majority group?
3. What can be done to balance the needs of diverse ethnic groups with the needs of California as a whole?

ENJOYING MEDIA

Movies to See and Web sites to Explore

Chicano/Latino Net   clnet.ucr.edu
The portal to networking in the Chicano/Chicana networks of California higher education including employment opportunities and cultural events.

University of California   universityofcalifornia.edu
The portal to the ten campuses of the University of California, the state's world renowned system of higher education.

California State University   calstate.edu
The portal to the California State University system's 23 campuses. These are the universities that train most of California's teachers, nurses, and many other professionals.

Multicultural Education   library.csustan.edu/lboyer/
                                            multicultural/main.htm
An introduction to the resources on the Web concerning multicultural education and diversity.

Spanglish, James L. Brooks, 2004
Comedy-drama about the cultural divide that occurs when a Mexican immigrant becomes housekeeper to a wealthy Jewish family in Malibu. A poignant illustration of the gaps between the haves and have-nots in California, and how human interactions can make a difference.

Grand Canyon, Lawrence Kasdan, 1991
A film about six diverse people living in Los Angeles during the 1990s. Shows the unlikely friendship of two men from different races and classes brought together when one finds himself in jeopardy in the other's rough neighborhood.

ENDNOTES

1. ACLU/SC Sues Upscale Coastal Resort for Treating Disabled Homeless People as Outlaws, March 6, 2009. http://www.aclu.org/disability/housing/38993prs20090306.html.
2. California School Apologizes for Illegally Banning Sixth Grader's Presentation on Harvey Milk, June 9, 2009. http://www.aclu.org/lgbt/youth/39803prs20090609.html.
3. "California Laws 1999," *Los Angeles Times*, January 1, 1999, p. A3.
4. Eric Bailey, "Central Valley Looking for Ways to Fight Air Pollution," *Los Angeles Times*, June 6, 2000, p. A3.
5. Joe Mozingo, "Officials Seek to Ease Fears on Plan to Curb Storm Runoff," *Los Angeles Times*, June 9, 2000, p. B3.
6. Jessie Mangaliman, "California Apologizes for Ill Treatment, Persecution of Chinese Immigrants," *San Jose Mercury News*, July 21, 2009. http://www.mercurynews.com/ci_12886337.
7. Dan Weikel, "$2.75 Million Ordered Paid to Minorities in Dockworker Case," *Los Angeles Times*, June 10, 2000, p. B1.
8. Dowell Myers and SungHo Ryu, "Aging Baby Boomers and the Generational Housing Bubble: Foresight and Mitigation of an Epic Transition," *Journal of the American Planning Association*, Vol. 74, No. 1, 2008. http://www.tandfonline.com/doi/full/10.1080/01944360701802006.
9. Armando Acuna, "Changes in State's Ethnic Balance Are Accelerating," *Los Angeles Times*, October 20, 1999, p. A3.
10. Jack Citrin and Benjamin Highton, "When the Sleeping Giant Is Awake," *California Journal*, Vol. 33, December 2002, p. 44.
11. Teresa Watanabe, "Chinese Take to U.S. Politics," *Los Angeles Times*, April 8, 2003, p. B1.
12. "State's Female Workers Paid Less than Men, Study Finds," *Los Angeles Times*, April 25, 1996, p. A21.
13. Jennifer Warren, "Plan Puts Female Inmates in Centers by Their Families," *Los Angeles Times*, February 11, 2006, p. A1.

CHAPTER FIVE

Media Influences and Interest Groups

California is the Wild, Wild West for influence-
peddling greased by campaign cash, self-dealing
and insider connections.

> —Jamie Court, President, Foundation for Taxpayer
> and Consumer Rights

In a democratic system, the attitudes of the public should be a primary basis for political decision making. These political attitudes are demonstrated in election results, public opinion polls, and in the inbox of every politician receiving input from constituents. Political views are influenced by numerous factors, including families, friends, religious institutions, schools, life experiences, and the activities of *interest groups*. But perhaps the greatest influence is the mass media, which bombards us with input on a daily basis. Modern media is fragmented into hundreds of thousands of elements: broadcast media now include hundreds of television channels and radio stations as well as thousands of Web sites, blogs, tweets, text messages, and other rapid-fire sources of information, all with varying degrees of validity. Add to this the more traditional print media, newspapers and magazines, and the variety of sources of information can become overwhelming. Finding accurate, useful information about California's political process is indeed a challenge.

THE MASS MEDIA: A MASSIVE INFLUENCE

Perhaps nothing better illustrates the power of the media to influence politics than the election of political newcomer Arnold Schwarzenegger as governor of California. Although he had no experience in office, his years starring as "the Terminator," who could solve problems with brute strength, apparently gave many California voters a sense of confidence in his political problem-solving ability. Entertainment merged with news coverage as the Schwarzenegger campaign caravan rolled through the state during the recall of 2003.

Fascination with "Arnold" created a brief media focus on state politics, but the broadcast media soon returned to its habits of occasional coverage of our state capitol. Most traditional broadcast media (television and radio) focus on national and international news, or churn out coverage of "news lite" stories of crime, freeway chases, and natural disasters. Ever-creative politicians have quickly adapted to the lack of news coverage of their activities by developing their own Web sites, blogs, e-mail blasts, tweets, and any form of media they think will enhance their image and future electability.

Image making is an expensive and essential business in California. The 2010 state election (Jerry Brown vs. Meg Whitman) broke all previous records for candidate spending, and no candidate for any office is considered serious by media or voters unless he or she has sufficient financial resources to run. Campaign funds are spent on various forms of communication, including all forms of media, plus "robocalls," text messages, e-mails, and even person-to-person precinct walks, all of which are coordinated by high-cost campaign consultants. The larger the electoral district, the less likely a campaign will include any personal contact but rather will depend on direct mail and mass media advertising. Critics charge that political information conveyed by the media emphasizes personality factors, attacks, and scandals rather than significant policy issues, but despite "peace pledges" and other gimmicks, most candidates eventually use negative campaigning to attract voter attention.

ECONOMIC INTEREST GROUPS: PRESSURE WHERE IT COUNTS

Organized *interest groups*—also known as lobbies—are also important in shaping public opinion and have been unusually influential in California politics. These groups often spend money through their *political action committees (PACs)*, which collect money from their members to spend on campaign contributions. In addition to official campaign contributions, organizations may also spend money on behalf of candidates or ballot measures that are known as *independent expenditures* and may also involve hundreds of millions of dollars. In addition to financial support, interest groups aid individual candidates by providing them with publicity and campaign workers. The most powerful groups are usually those with the most financial resources, including the majority of business interests and some of the larger unions, such as those for public school teachers and state prison guards. When a group supports a successful candidate, it gains better access to that politician than most other individuals ever have.

Interest groups generally avoid direct affiliation with any political party, preferring instead to work with whichever politician is in office. Business groups usually prefer to help elect Republicans, whereas labor groups prefer Democrats. The influence of various interest groups is indicated, in part, by their wealth and the number of people who belong to or are employed by their organizations. Nearly all of California's most profitable corporations, including oil companies, insurance giants, utilities, banks, and telecommunications companies, are linked together in pressure groups such as the California Manufacturers and Technology Association, the Western States Petroleum Association, and the California Cable and Telecommunications Association.[1] Other major *private-sector* players in the lobbying game are the California Nations Indian Gaming Association, the California Association of Realtors, the California Medical Association, the Trial Lawyers Association, and the Agricultural Producers. The California Teachers Association, the California Correctional Peace Officers Association, the California State Employees Association, the California Labor Federation, and many other groups represent labor interests, though not necessarily in a unified manner. These same business and labor groups work to get laws passed that help them and to influence the state budget so that its outcome favors their members.

Repeated attempts to curb the spending and influence of special interests have had limited success. Under the free speech rights guaranteed by the U.S. Constitution, courts have repeatedly ruled that limits on campaign contributions are a limit on free speech. This enables large organizations as well as affluent individuals to continue dominating campaign fund-raising (Table 5.1). Californians may be dismayed by the role of huge campaign dollars, but they have not figured out how to end this.

TABLE 5.1

Political Contributions to State-Level Candidates and Ballot Measures, 2010

Sector	Amount Contributed	Number of Contributions
Candidates (to themselves)	$207,338,107	3,927
Labor	$76,457,711	10,056
Energy and Natural Resources	$72,333,345	3,623
Finance, Insurance, and Real Estate	$62,301,731	10,644
Ideology/Single Issue	$30,831,090	1,147
Communications and Electronics	$30,101,606	4,749
General Business	$29,601,840	5,333
Government Agencies, Education, other	$25,930,205	5,295
Political Parties	$24,603,809	3,108
Health Industries	$18,531,394	9,312
Lawyers and Lobbyists	$14,223,529	14,213
Agriculture	$6,370,199	3,759
Construction	$4,657,759	2,071
Transportation	$2,915,278	1,353

Top Donors in Selected Categories

Sector	Contributor	Amount Contributed
Energy	Pacific Gas & Electric Co.	$46 million
Insurance	Mercury General Corp	$16 million
Political Party	California Democratic Party	$17 million
Public Labor unions	California Teachers Association	$15 million

Source: National Institute on Money in State Politics: Follow the Money, 2010, http://www.follow themoney.org

OTHER INTEREST GROUPS: LESS MONEY BUT STILL A VOICE

In addition to the business, professional, and labor groups that spend money to elect candidates and later make contact with elected officials to share their views, California's political process has enabled less-affluent interest groups to develop and participate. Such groups, discussed in Chapter 6, include those representing various ethnic communities, environmental organizations such as the Planning and Conservation League, Children Now (which concerns itself with the needs of youth), and single-issue groups such as the California Abortion Rights Action League, Handgun Control, the Fund for Animals, and Surfriders (whose primary interest is in protecting beaches). These groups may not provide much campaign funding, but they often offer volunteers whose election support activities gain credibility for the organization.

In addition to an enormous array of nongovernmental lobbies, government agencies also lobby for their concerns, with numerous cities, counties, and *special districts*, such as water agencies and school districts, employing paid lobbyists in Sacramento. These government entities often seek funding or other legislative support from the state.

LOBBYISTS IN ACTION: A HIGH-SKILL, HIGH-PAY CAREER

The term *lobbying* arose when those who wanted to influence elected officials would congregate in the lobbies of government buildings and wait to speak with a politician about their concerns. California's lobbyists, like those around the nation, gradually developed a pattern of wining and dining the politicians as well as giving them gifts and campaign contributions. Periodic scandals in which lobbyists and legislators are convicted of crimes involving trading votes for financial rewards create public demand for reform of the lobbying industry. The 1974 Political Reform Initiative requires each lobbyist to file monthly reports showing income, expenditures, and steps taken to influence government action. This initiative also created the Fair Political Practices Commission (FPPC), which oversees campaigns and lobbying and monitors any possible wrongdoing by candidates or PACs. The Online Disclosure Act (1997) requires all lobbying expenditures to be posted online at http://www.cal-access.ss.ca.gov (a site located within the secretary of state's Web site).

The most recent successful effort to control campaign spending was Proposition 34 (November 2000). This ballot measure was written and passed by the legislature and then approved by voters. Many political experts question whether the provisions are strict enough and criticize the measure for leaving too many loopholes for wealthy special interests. Meanwhile, the size of average contributions to state Assembly and Senate campaigns increased by one-third.[2] Proposition 34 does not control spending by independent expenditure campaigns, in which special-interest groups run ads and send mailers without coordinating their effort with the candidate.

In addition to helping favorable politicians get elected, lobbyists perform an assortment of tasks to achieve their organization's goals.

Many lobbyists are former lawmakers or legislative aides, whose personal contacts enable them to work successfully in the halls of power. They earn substantial salaries for handling the following:

1. Campaign efforts (primarily financial contributions) to elect sympathetic candidates, especially incumbents.

2. Testimony for or against bills being considered by legislative committees.

3. Informal contacts with lawmakers for purposes of providing them with information, statistical data, and expert opinions on pending legislation.

4. Ads and announcements in newspapers, on Web sites, and through direct mail, which appeal to the public to take a position and convey their views to elected officials.

5. Sponsorship of initiative or referendum petitions to put propositions on the ballot for the approval of the voters.

6. Encouragement of interest group members to write letters or send e-mails to lawmakers regarding particular bills.

7. Organization of protest marches and other forms of public demonstrations.

8. Favorable publicity and endorsements for cooperative lawmakers inserted in the internal publications of the organization.

9. Attempts to influence the appointment (by the governor) of sympathetic judges and administrative officials.

With the passage of *term limits* (Proposition 140) in 1990, the influence of lobbyists has changed. Before term limits, lobbyists could develop ongoing friendships with legislators, who often spent decades in office. Now, legislators rotate out of office frequently, and lobbyists must quickly develop relationships with newly elected officials and their new staff members. Those newly elected officials may be more susceptible to lobbyists, because lobbyists have much more experience in Sacramento than most new legislators.

Because lobbying still determines the outcome of almost all legislation, Californians who realize how much political decisions can affect their daily lives usually become interested in tracking the impact of lobbying on their elected officials. This involves checking campaign donation records as well as legislators' voting records in order to find out how a particular group has influenced a specific legislator. Two excellent sources of information are the secretary of state's Cal-Access Web site and http://www.followthemoney.org. The best solution for individuals interested in more direct involvement may be to join the interest groups that reflect their values and political concerns. Many lobbies are open groups that welcome new members. These include organizations involved with environmental

DEBATING THE ISSUES

INTEREST GROUPS

Viewpoint: Interest groups should remain free from restrictions and engage in campaign contributions and political advocacy in order to ensure multiple perspectives in political decision making.

- Freedom of speech means for everyone, including well-financed groups that may have messages to convey to the public or to elected officials.
- When multiple and diverse interest groups participate in politics, all views ultimately are represented in the dialogue.

Viewpoint: Interest groups must be carefully regulated by government to ensure that well-financed organizations do not dominate the political process. Campaigns should be publicly funded to avoid all forms of interest group financial influence.

- Interest groups vary hugely in their financial resources and the big money players must not be allowed to dominate the political dialogue.
- Reducing interest group dollars and using public dollars for campaigns enables more diverse candidates to enter politics.
- Money is power, and that power must be balanced by fair standards.

Ask Yourself: Am I represented by any organized interest group? If not, what can I do to have a voice in the political process?

issues, ethnic concerns, health care, and many more. (See Appendix A for a directory of organizations anyone can join.) Members receive updates from lobbyists indicating what legislation is being considered and how the individual can phone or write in a timely, informed manner. (See Appendix B for information about contacting elected officials.) Any individual Californian can write a letter or send an e-mail, but the most effective political action comes through organized groups.

QUESTIONS TO CONSIDER

Using Your Text and Your Own Experiences

1. In how many ways do mass media influence political attitudes? Give examples of those influences. Remember that media include both the information media and the entertainment media.

2. What makes a special-interest group powerful? Are there problems with how much power some of these groups have?

3. Is personal wealth an essential ingredient for individual political influence? If you are not wealthy, what can you do to have a voice in California's political process?

ENJOYING MEDIA

Movies to See and Web sites to Explore

California Chamber of Commerce   calchamber.com
California's small businesses are represented by the State Chamber of Commerce, a powerful voice in Sacramento.

California Labor Federation   calaborfed.org
The coalition of most labor unions in the state is very active in Sacramento.

California League of Conservation Voters   ecovote.org
Environmental issues are the core of this effective political advocacy group.

Faculty Association of California Community Colleges   faccc.org
This active Sacramento lobby represents Community College faculty from the 110 California Community Colleges.

Center for Responsive Politics   opensecrets.org
(tracking money in campaigns)
This organization's Web site can help you figure out who gives what to which politicians.

The China Syndrome, James Bridges, 1979
A thriller about corporate cover-ups when a reporter tries to investigate a dangerous incident at a California nuclear power plant. One of the first movies to explore environmental issues, the role of the media, and the power of corporations.

Thank You for Smoking, Jason Reitman, 2005
An inside look at the life of a tobacco lobbyist, whose job includes a trip to Hollywood to promote smoking in studio films. Fictional, yet almost like reality when it comes to the power of big money interests.

ENDNOTES

1. "Top 10 Lobbyist Employers Ranked from High to Low," Secretary of State 3rd Quarter Report, January 1, 1999–September 30,1999. http://www.ss.ca.gov.
2. Raymond J. La Raja and Dorie Apollonio, "Term Limits Affect Legislators' Fund Raising Prowess," *Institute of Governmental Studies Public Affairs Report*, University of California, Vol. 40, No. 5, September 1999, p. 3.

CHAPTER SIX

Political Parties and Other Voluntary Organizations

The success of the Republican and Democratic parties is gauged by how they do at election time; electing their candidates is their primary focus.

—Ken deBow and John Syer, political scientists

Although most Californians who are registered voters belong to one of the two major parties, a substantial minority have chosen other voting affiliations. About 20 percent of California voters belong to no party ("decline to state" or *unaffiliated* registration status), and another 5 percent are members of one of the four minor parties, with these numbers increasing each year. Many citizen activists remain almost entirely separate from party organizations and yet are immersed in the *grassroots* political process through an enormous variety of voluntary associations, some of which, like many Parent Teacher Associations (PTAs), Neighborhood Councils, and homeowner groups, have become highly politicized. Activities that used to require volunteers with time and energy and little political awareness now require participants who understand the intimate links between one's neighborhood problems or local school issues and the larger California political and budget process. Parents of children in poor performance schools, homeowners concerned about graffiti, and beach lovers whose shores are polluted are among many Californians whose political involvement begins when they collect signatures for ballot initiatives or lobby public officials in an effort to resolve their particular problems.

Meanwhile, despite the small numbers of Californians who participate directly in their political parties or feel any special enthusiasm for either party, *party affiliations* are reflected in the voting patterns of legislators and the track records of governors. On many issues of major public concern, such as traffic and transportation, criminal justice, the environment, and funding for education, the votes of individual legislators may depend more on party allegiance than on any other factor.

DO PARTIES MATTER? THE VOTERS' PERSPECTIVE

California's tradition of minimal loyalty to either of the two major parties has roots in the state constitution's rules regarding state employment and elections. California's *civil service system* fills 98 percent of all state government jobs on the basis of competitive exams, thereby reducing the number of jobs that can be used as *patronage* to reward supporters of the winning party. Local offices (including city, county, and education boards) and all judicial elections are *nonpartisan*, with candidates listed by name and occupation, with no mention of party affiliation. The ballot format itself, known as the *office-block ballot*, lists candidates under the heading of the office being contested rather than in columns divided according to party, and thus encourages voters to concentrate on individual candidates rather than voting a straight party ticket. The nonpartisan nature of most California politics is best understood in terms of the fact that only 179 of the 19,279 elective offices throughout the state are *partisan*.[1]

Although the parties are not as well organized or as meaningful to voters as they are in some other states, Californians display some partisan loyalty. Many voters registered in a party still vote for their party's candidates without much thought, and the enormous amounts of campaign funds spent on media are often aimed at the 25 percent

---

COMPARED TO CALIFORNIA

VOTER REGISTRATION RULES IN SELECTED STATES

California: Voters must register at least 15 days before the election in order to vote.

Idaho, Maine, Minnesota, New Hampshire, Wisconsin, and Wyoming: Voters may register to vote on Election Day.

Source: The Center for Information and Research on Civic Learning and Engagement (CIRCLE), http://www.civicyouth.org/Map.htm

Think Critically: Does voter participation improve if people can register to vote on the day of the election? Why might some people wait until then to decide to vote?

TABLE 6.1
California Voter Registration Patterns, 1950–2011

	Democrat (%)	Republican (%)	Other (%)	Decline to State (%)
1950	58	35	1	4
1960	57	38	1	3
1970	55	39	2	4
1980	53	34	3	9
1990	49	39	3	9
2000	46	35	5	14
2011	44	31	5	20

Source: California Secretary of State.

of voters who are not registered with either major party and therefore are considered *swing votes*. Recent Field Poll data indicate that many of the unaffiliated voters are Latinos and Asians with moderate views; Republican Party registration is nearly 80 percent white and Democrats are 55 percent white.[2] Table 6.1 shows historic declines in voter affiliation with the two major parties.

Although voters are less tied to parties than in the past, party leaders and elected officials can be intensely partisan, as exemplified by the annual state budget battles between Sacramento's "Dems" and "Reps." Differences between Democrats and Republicans show up very clearly on matters such as taxation, aid to low-income Californians, and other major fiscal concerns. As the battle over the 2011 state budget indicates, the party caucuses remained unified: Republicans determined to prevent any form of tax increase and Democrats fighting against cuts to education and social services. Thanks to Proposition 25 (2010), for the first time in decades, the state budget could be passed by a simple majority. However, taxes may not be imposed without a full two-thirds majority, so the Republican minority defeated all tax proposals and the resulting state budget imposed deep cuts to public education, state parks, services to the disabled, and health care for low-income children.

With all the partisan dissension, it is perhaps no wonder that many citizens register their disapproval by refusing to vote at all or by registering to vote without affiliating with either major party. In the 2010 *gubernatorial* election, only 44 percent of eligible voters bothered to vote.[3]

MINOR PARTIES: ALTERNATIVE POLITICAL VOICES

Although the state constitution makes it very difficult for minor parties to get on the ballot, California voters manage to show their frustration with the two major parties. Between 1966 and 2011, the percentage of voters registered as either Democrats or Republicans dropped from 94 percent to 75 percent.[4] Among the other party options are the Libertarian (belief in individual freedom, *minimalist* government), American Independent (antigay, antiabortion, antitax, pro-God), Greens (environmental issues, social justice), and Peace and Freedom (socialism, democracy, feminism). To attain qualified *ballot status*, these parties must get 1 percent of registered voters to write in the new party in the "Other" space on the voter registration form or get 10 percent of voters to sign petitions. They remain official parties with ballot status as long as any of their candidates for statewide office receives 2 percent of the vote.

Some of the parties currently attempting to get qualified for ballot status include the Christian Party, the Utopia Manifesto Party, the We Like Women Party, the Constitution Party, and the Reform Party.[5] At the moment, none of the minor parties have a candidate in state level office, but there are a handful of Libertarians and Greens serving on local city councils and special district boards around the state.

PARTY ORGANIZATION: WHO MAKES THE RULES?

California's parties are regulated by both state law and their own internal guidelines. The two major parties have similar general structures: a state central committee and 58 *county committees*. The most powerful nonelected official in each party is the state party chair, although this individual is rarely well known by the general public. Beyond these two committees, much of party organization is left to each party. Democrats have organized themselves into Assembly district committees, whereas Republicans rely primarily on county committees for their local activities (see Figure 6.1). These activities include recruiting candidates, raising money, registering voters, and supporting party nominees in general elections.

This level of political activity involves only a small fraction of the population. Of the 20 million Californians eligible to vote, only 73 percent have registered, and even fewer actually vote. California's new "top two" primary system could perhaps encourage more *unaffiliated* voters to participate and may reduce party influence in elections. Even before voter registration in the two major parties dropped to its current low (75 percent of registered voters), California's parties were designed to be weak. In order to overcome the structural antiparty bias of the state constitution, the two major parties attempt to create stronger internal structures by promoting clubs or caucuses. The Republican Party's very conservative Young Americans for Freedom (YAF) has an historic role, while the moderate and well-financed Republicans for a New Majority claim increasing influence. Democrats stay close to their liberal roots through the California Democratic Council, the

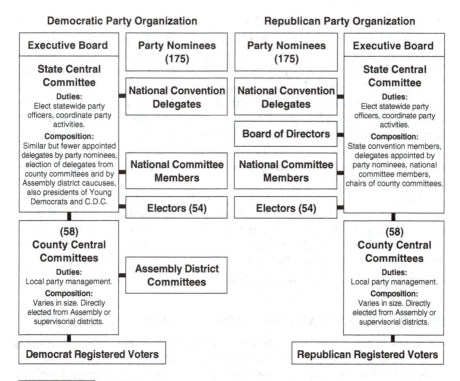

FIGURE 6.1   **Political Party Organization**

Source: California Government and Politics Annual.

party's largest club. Other small groupings include the Log Cabin Club (Republican gay rights group) and the Democrats for Israel. In general, these internal organizations have only an indirect impact on the larger political process.

Perhaps because parties are not very powerful, and because most party activists are unknown and unrecognized, many Californians choose to be politically active without being involved in parties.

OUTSIDE PARTIES: NONPARTISAN POLITICAL ORGANIZATIONS

Outside the party structure and party-oriented organizations are a multitude of grassroots groupings that provide the genuine political focus of many Californians. Perhaps the growing popularity of such groups reflects the historical weakness of parties and the current low profiles of the partisan organizations. Or perhaps the issues that confront Californians daily are best approached through *issue-oriented organizations* with no absolute loyalty to any party.

For those concerned with environmental protection, groups such as Heal the Bay (based in Santa Monica), the Labor/Community Strategy Center (in Los Angeles), the League of Conservation Voters (statewide), and numerous other local and regional groups are in constant need of volunteers' time, energy, and money. For women seeking greater representation, the California chapters of the National Women's Political Caucus, the California Abortion Rights Action League, and the Los Angeles–based Fund for a Feminist Majority all raise money and organize volunteers to get women into office as well as to elect men sympathetic to feminist concerns.

African American and Latino activists are often involved in California affiliates of the Southern Christian Leadership Conference, the National Association for the Advancement of Colored People, the Southwest Voter Registration and Education Project, the Mexican American Political Association, and the Mexican American Legal Defense and Education Fund, all of which encourage minority involvement in both electoral politics and community issues. Asian Americans, rivaling Latinos as the fastest-growing minority group, derive much of their political clout from the Asian Pacific American Legal Center, the Asian American Action Fund, and the Asian

DEBATING THE ISSUES

POLITICAL PARTIES

Viewpoint: The two major political parties are losing members and political strength because they do not represent the views of voters. Laws should be changed to allow minor parties a real chance to win elections.

- The two major parties do not reflect the political views of many people.
- Voter participation would increase if more parties had a real chance to elect candidates.
- Multiparty systems work well in many stable democracies.

Viewpoint: The two major parties remain useful ways for voters to choose candidates, and the two-party system should be reinforced.

- Multiple parties could confuse voters and reduce voter turnout.
- Some third parties encourage extremism in politics.
- Third parties can be "spoilers" that change electoral outcomes for the worse.

Ask Yourself: Do I know about the political party options beyond the two major parties? Might there be a better "fit" for me than being in a major party?

Pacific Policy Institute. All of these groups concern themselves with the ongoing issues of minorities, including access to employment, education, and housing, as well as adequate representation in politics and media.

Other forms of voluntary associations that bring people together include the Bus Riders Union (supporting low-cost public transportation), California Bicycle Coalition, local homeowner and resident associations, Neighborhood Councils, and numerous ad hoc committees that come together for short-term purposes, such as planting trees or preventing unwanted development projects. California's organized historic preservationists battle to protect architectural and cultural landmarks from demolition, while Neighborhood Watch committees, formed by small groups of neighbors in coordination with local police departments, carry out important tasks such as painting out graffiti, reporting abandoned cars, and keeping track of crime. Voluntary groups whose issues become the focus of widespread concern can ultimately create major changes, such as the "Three Strikes, You're Out" laws that exist in part owing to the political organizing done by families damaged by violent crime.

Californians in search of the California Dream have two clear options: They can "cocoon" themselves into the privacy of their homes and try to block out the social stresses around them, or they can join other concerned people to work toward improving the quality of life. Literally hundreds of organizations exist through the volunteer efforts of people who want to make a difference. The only limits on political participation are the time and energy of people, who may find that their voluntary political participation soon begins to feel essential. Once the connections between individual problems and the political process are made, it becomes difficult to return to a narrow, nonpolitical life.

QUESTIONS TO CONSIDER

Using Your Text and Your Own Experiences

1. What are some issues in everyday life that are impacted by political decision makers? Discuss the importance of understanding this connection between daily life and politics.

2. How important are political parties? Why is there an increase in people registering under "decline to state" or in a minor party? What other type of organization can people join to express their political concerns?

3. Research the current minor parties, their philosophies, and their leaders. Can you create the framework for another party that should exist in California?

ENJOYING MEDIA

Movies to See and Web sites to Explore

League of Women Voters of California ca.lwv.org
A nonpartisan organization that attempts to keep politics accessible to the public.

Young Americans for Freedom (Republican) yaf.org
A conservative group that often recruits on college campuses.

Young Democrats of California (Democratic) youngdems.org
Young Democrats include both college students and young professionals.

Green Party (California) cagreens.org
The party that focuses on environment and social justice.

Libertarian Meetup (open meetings) libertarian.meetup.com
Libertarians believe in minimal government and have an informal structure for getting involved.

Rated 'R': Republicans in Hollywood, directed by Jesse Moss, 2004
This one-hour documentary looks behind the silver screen and examines the political truth about conservatives in Tinseltown. The film presents Hollywood's most prominent and outspoken conservatives and, through revealing verite scenes, documents the political activities of Hollywood's revitalized Right.

Bulworth, Warren Beatty, 1998
A cynical comic look at the political process in which a California Senator falls in love with an African American woman from South Los Angeles and begins to campaign using hip-hop music and poetry. His statements portray both major parties as corrupt, and he depicts the entire system as money-driven.

ENDNOTES

1. David G Savage, "Nonpartisan Vote Challenge Voided," *Los Angeles Times*, June 18, 1991, p. A3.
2. Field Poll, "California Opinion Index, The Changing California Electorate," August 2009. http://www.field.com/fieldpollonline/subscribers/COI-09-August-California-Electorate.pdf.
3. California Secretary of State, 2010. http://www.sos.ca.gov/elections/sov/2010-general/complete-sov.pdf.
4. California Secretary of State, http://www.sos.ca.gov.
5. California Secretary of State Web site, "Political Bodies Attempting to Qualify for the June 2012 Ballot." http://www.sos.ca.gov/elections/ror/ror-pages/15day-stwdsp-09/non-qual-chairs.pdf.

CHAPTER SEVEN

Campaigns and Elections: Too Many?

Money is the mother's milk of politics.
—Jess Unruh, Former California Assembly Speaker

Public officials are normally chosen in a two-step process involving both primary and runoff or general elections. Beginning in June 2012, Californians no longer have *partisan* primaries for state offices, but instead now use the "voter-nominated" or "top-two" system, which allows for the two highest vote-getters to go into the general election even if both are from the same political party. In this primary system, which covers all legislative, executive, and Congressional races, all candidates for a given elected office appear on one list for voters, and all voters receive identical ballots and vote for any one of the candidates on the list. Candidates may choose not to indicate their party affiliation in these new "top-two" elections. It is believed that this system will continue to diminish the power of California's political parties and may also increase voter participation among *unaffiliated* (no party) voters.

Any registered voter may run for an office in the primary by filing a declaration of candidacy with the county clerk at least 69 days before the election, paying a filing fee (unless granted an exemption based on inability to pay), and submitting a petition with the signatures of from 20 to 500 registered voters, depending on the office sought.

In local, nonpartisan elections, such as for county, city, or education board positions, some jurisdictions have sub-districts or wards in which one candidate must get a true *majority* (50 percent plus one) in order to win. In these cases, if no candidate in the nonpartisan primary receives a majority, the two with the most votes face one another in a later *runoff election*.

For these jurisdictions, an alternative to the primary-runoff system is Instant Runoff Voting (IRV), also known as Ranked Choice voting, now being used in San Francisco and under consideration in Los Angeles, Long Beach, and other cities in order to save election costs and increase voter participation.[1] Smaller counties, cities, or education districts that hold *at-large* elections rarely have runoffs, because the top two or three candidates for city council or school board win, although none may have gained an actual majority of votes.

In general elections, held in early November of even-numbered years for state and national offices, the ballot includes the top two vote-getters for each office (except for United States President, which still involves a modified *closed primary* in which the candidate in each party who receives a *plurality* of votes becomes the party's nominee) and all propositions that have qualified for that ballot. Most voters still go to the *polls* to vote, but an increasing number take advantage of *vote-by-mail* (VBM) ballots to vote at home and mail their ballots, thus saving the time it may take to vote in person. Some small jurisdictions are experimenting with an all-mail election to save the costs of setting up voting locations.[2]

CALIFORNIA POLITICIANS: SEE HOW THEY RUN

It is relatively easy to run for office in California, but to win requires a combination of campaign ingredients that may be difficult to assemble. One of the most important is an electable candidate. Name recognition is important, and the occasional political success of a well-known actor always reminds us that voters like to vote for familiar names, and not necessarily on the basis of political background or qualifications.

Familiar political names can also develop in ambitious families. In Los Angeles, there is the Hahn family (father Kenny was a county supervisor, son Jim was mayor, and daughter Janice served on the city council before being elected to the House of Representatives), and in the Inland Empire, there is the Calderon family, with brothers Tom, Ron, and Charles all serving in the legislature at various times. Similarly, the widows of elected officials are often chosen to replace their husbands, in part because of name recognition. Both Mary Bono Mack (R, Palm Springs) and Lois Capps (D, Santa Barbara) were elected to complete the congressional terms of their deceased husbands and were then reelected on their own in subsequent years. And California is home to the first "sister team" in Congress, Loretta and Linda Sanchez, both of whom serve Southern California districts.

MONEY AND POLITICS: THE VITAL LINK

In part because name recognition is so important, and because it takes a lot of money to create that recognition, California campaigns are now so expensive that one of the greatest dangers to democratic politics is that races are often won by the biggest spenders, not necessarily the best candidates. Until recently, *incumbents* typically had the advantage in terms of finances and name recognition, but both *term limits* and the recent trend toward extremely wealthy individuals spending millions to create name identification have altered the situation. Of course, spending $144 million of her personal fortune did not help Meg Whitman get elected governor, but campaign strategists explain that personal scandal (her allegedly undocumented household help) outweighs even vast sums of money.

Both incumbents and *challengers* channel many of their campaign dollars to highly paid consultants, who push their clients to raise even more money in order to pay other campaign costs. Much of the money is spent on broadcast media including all the new varieties. The increasing use of the e-mail blasts, text messaging, and tweets to promote campaigns is relatively inexpensive but still reaches only a segment of the public, so most campaign strategists do not rely on any one technology to mount a successful campaign. Although TV ads are not efficient because they reach so many nonvoters, they are still essential components of most statewide campaigns while local candidates try to utilize local cable channels to target voters.

In addition to broadcast media purchases, campaign costs include various consultants' fees, polling costs, and direct mail to voters. Direct mail has become an intricate business in which experts help candidates mail persuasive literature to *target audiences*. In tight races, where *swing voters* may make the difference, one brochure targets conservatives while another appeals to liberals. Another frequent strategy is to avoid mentioning party affiliation in order to appeal to the many Californians who are registered as *decline to state*. Like other Americans, Californians turn out to vote in proportion to the amount of media attention and controversy generated by an election as well as in relation to how "turned off" they are by negative campaign tactics. Some candidates benefit from a small turnout and help create that outcome by using ads that are intentionally ugly.

Campaign resources now come in two basic categories: (1) direct campaign contributions to candidates as well as to ballot measures, including those office-seekers who self-fund as well as those supported by individuals and interest groups and (2) *independent expenditures*, money spent by many of the same interest groups that have already contributed to a candidate but who wish to spend more to assist their chosen candidate. In 2010, the total of campaign contributions and independent expenditures for California's elections was nearly three-quarters of a billion dollars ("Billion" with a B). Many police officers, teachers, firefighters, and mental health workers in the state would gladly have seen those same hundreds of millions spent on the services they strive to provide. Despite the periodic voter-approved campaign reforms, money is still the major factor in most elections.

The hundreds of millions of campaign dollars come from a variety of sources. The Fair Political Practices Commission, set up by voters in 1974 through the initiative process, keeps records of donations. The pattern of donations continues to show high spending by special-interest groups, with top campaign spenders including virtually the same list of pressure groups that also lobby Sacramento throughout the year: oil companies, utilities, tribal gaming, telecommunications businesses, banks, agribusinesses, insurance corporations, doctors, lawyers, labor unions, teachers, and prison guards. Political fund-raisers report that an average of 85 percent of the money raised for candidates is the cost of doing business for special-interest groups, with the remaining 15 percent being "love money" from friends and family.[3]

Although most campaigning is done with dollars, California voters occasionally get a taste of the more personal campaign styles of the past. During election season, those who are registered to vote may answer the doorbell and find a campaign staff member or volunteer coming to chat. Occasionally, the candidate actually visits in person; however, only a candidate who is very dedicated or reasonably well-to-do can afford to quit work to campaign on a daily basis. Automated phone calls (robocalls) or calls made by volunteers are also used, with calls placed to those whose voting record indicates they are likely to vote.

ELECTIONS WITHOUT CANDIDATES: DIRECT DEMOCRACY

Our federal system is a *representative democracy* in which voters elect officials to make decisions for them. The federal system has no form of direct citizen decision making: Every decision is made by elected officials. However, states may choose to develop their own forms of *direct democracy*, in which voters may bypass elected officials to make laws themselves or even to remove elected officials from office. California's direct democracy was created by the Progressives of the early 1900s as part of their strategy to bring political power back to the people, and Californians have made ample use of this opportunity. California's constitution ensures that the state's voters can make laws, amend the state constitution, repeal laws, or recall elected officials through the ballot box.

The most commonly used of the three forms of direct democracy—the initiative, referendum, and recall—is the *initiative* (see Figure 7.1).

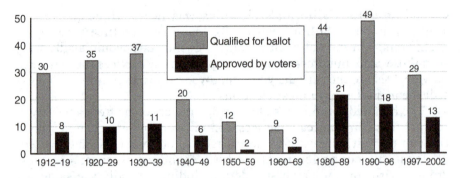

FIGURE 7.1 **California Initiatives, 1912–2002**

The initiative permits registered voters to place a proposed law, or *statute*, on the ballot through petition signatures equal to 5 percent of the votes cast in the last election for governor (the current required number of valid signatures is 504,760). Similarly, voters may propose amendments to the state constitution (which requires 8 percent to get onto the ballot, or 807,615 signatures). Petition circulators are given 150 days in which to gather signatures. The secretary of state receives the petitions and evaluates whether enough valid signatures have been collected. If there are enough signatures, the measure is given a proposition number and can be approved by a simple majority in the next election. Because of the high costs of qualifying an initiative and promoting its passage, the large majority of initiatives on the ballot are written and promoted by organized special-interest groups, which usually pay professional signature gatherers to qualify propositions to appear on the ballot.

Less frequently used are *referendums*, of which there are two types. One type allows voters to repeal a law passed by the legislature. Owing to the requirement that all signatures must be gathered within a mere 90 days of the legislation's passage, this type of referendum has rarely appeared on the ballot. The second type of referendum is one submitted to the voters by the legislature rather than by petition; this is most frequently used for *bond measures*.

The third component of direct democracy, the *recall*, is a device by which voters can petition for a special election to remove an official from office before his or her term has expired. Unlike impeachment, which is initiated by the elected legislative body, recall efforts begin with petitions by registered voters (often mobilized by a special-interest group's dollars). Recall attempts are more common than actual recall elections: prior to 2003, there were 35 recall efforts against California governors, but none obtained enough signatures to get on the ballot. Then the recall drive against Gray Davis, fueled largely by Republican Darryl Issa's millions, obtained the required 900,000 signatures and thus succeeded in getting onto the ballot. A recall petition normally requires the valid signatures of 12–25 percent of those who voted in the last election; if that requirement is met, anyone may file to run for that office. Voters must then vote on whether or not to recall the official and on which of the other candidates to elect to fill the possible vacancy. There can be no runoff; the candidate with the most votes wins the position.

DIRECT DEMOCRACY: PROS AND CONS

The Progressives intended that the initiative, referendum, and recall would help citizens make policy directly or remove incompetent officials, thus counteracting the corruption of state or local officials who might be too dependent on powerful special interests. Instead, those same special interests have grown sophisticated in their use of these mechanisms to achieve their goals. Because the signatures of over 504,000 registered voters are necessary to place a statutory initiative on the ballot (and over 807,000 are required for a constitutional amendment) and because signature gatherers must get twice as many as required in order to offset the many invalid signatures found by the secretary of state, it can easily require over $1 million just to qualify a measure. The costs to publicize the measure (by those favoring and those opposing it) can go into the multimillion-dollar range—just for one controversial proposition. Another problem is that there are no limits on the number of propositions per election—voters may become overwhelmed by the work required to read and evaluate dozens of ballot measures. Yet another problem with initiatives is that measures may pass by large margins and yet still have unconstitutional elements which the courts then negate. As to the recall, critics suggest that it can be used unfairly against a competent but unpopular official.

Most political experts and politicians believe that California's direct democracy needs reform. Ideas for improvement include imposing a legal review of propositions before they are circulated for signatures, changing the time limits for signature gathering, making it easier for the legislature to amend initiatives without returning to the voters, requiring more disclosure of who is financing a ballot measure, and enforcing the requirement that initiatives deal with only one subject.

Perhaps one reason that it is so difficult to reform the direct democracy process is that it still serves one function: to remove power from elected officials and grant that power to the voters. In some sense, direct democracy adds a fourth element to the checks and balances of the three branches of government, one in which the voters themselves find a voice—a voice that may differ enormously from the ones emanating from the halls of government in California.

DEBATING THE ISSUES

DIRECT DEMOCRACY

Viewpoint: Direct democracy is a wonderful tool for the people to oversee the political process.

- There is nothing as purely democratic as a vote of the people.
- Direct democracy ensures that elected officials do not get too powerful.
- Direct democracy increases voter interest and voter turnout.

Viewpoint: Direct democracy has become a tool of big money interests and no longer represents the people.

- California's direct democracy has become a big money project that has little to do with representing the will of the people.
- Many ballot decisions made by voters turn out to be mistakes for the state.
- Voters get confused and discouraged by the number, length, and complexity of ballot measures.

Ask Yourself: What do I like about direct democracy? What would I like to see changed?

CLEANING UP POLITICS: CAMPAIGN REFORM

Every few years yet another campaign reform initiative seems to appear on the California ballot. Often, two conflicting initiatives may deal with the same issue. Over time, voters have approved restrictions on transfers of funds between candidates, required reporting of donations to the Fair Political Practices Commission, and imposed strict limits on the amount

COMPARED TO CALIFORNIA

DIRECT DEMOCRACY: CALIFORNIA AND THE UNITED STATES

U.S. elections: No direct democracy.

California: Initiative, referendum, and recall enacted for California and its counties and cities in 1911 under Governor Hiram Johnson.

Think Critically: Our federal government never asks for a public vote on policy decisions. Is it a better system to rely on elected representatives to make decisions for us? Or is California's direct democracy better?

a lobbyist can spend to wine and dine an elected official. Yet it seems that each time voters say yes to a reform, the unintended consequences of the law show up in later years and demonstrate the difficulty of separating money from politics. Recent efforts include the California Clean Money Initiative, which would have created public financing, and was defeated, and a follow-up measure calling for a pilot program to use public financing for the Secretary of State race in 2014 and 2018.

THE CHANGING ELECTORATE: WHO VOTES AND WHO DOESN'T

With about one-quarter of the population being immigrants from other nations,[4] California's pool of eligible voters is proportionately smaller than that in many other states. Traditionally, voter turnout in California is similar to that in other states: many fewer people vote than are eligible. Nonvoters include the "contented apathetics," who just aren't interested in politics because they see no need to be; people who are devoting all their time to economic survival and don't have time or energy to become informed citizens; and those who are politically alienated and believe their vote makes no difference.[5] Voters tend to be more affluent, better educated, and older than average, leaving many younger, poorer, and less educated Californians underrepresented in the electoral process. In California, the electorate is much "whiter" than the population, with about 70 percent of voters being white, even though whites make up somewhat less than half the population (see Table 7.1). Research indicates that the way political district boundaries are determined may also influence voter turnout among Latinos and blacks, with higher participation in districts where they are the majority of voters.[6] Until ethnic minorities and lower-income citizens vote in larger numbers, the trend toward a multicultural state with a *monocultural electorate* will continue.

TABLE 7.1

Voter Ethnicity in California General Elections

Year	Latino (%)	White (%)	Asian (%)	Black (%)	Other (%)
2010	18	66	7	6	3
2006	14	72	5	6	3
2000	14	71	6	7	2
1996	12	76	4	6	1
1994	9	77	4	8	2
1990	4	82	4	8	2

Source: California Journal, September 2002; PPIC 2006, 2009, 2010.

Having a real democracy requires time and energy from ordinary citizens. Otherwise, the few who bother to vote will exercise disproportionate power, and those they elect may feel responsible to fewer people rather than to society as a whole.

QUESTIONS TO CONSIDER

Using Your Text and Your Own Experiences

1. Discuss the relationship between money and politics. What forms of political activity and access are available to people who do not have large sums to give to candidates or PACs?

2. Debate the pros and cons of our three direct democracy mechanisms. Would California be better off without them or with a modified version?

3. Take a class survey. Pair up voters with nonvoters to discuss the issue of voter participation. Does your classroom reflect the monocultural electorate or a changing electorate? Can voters persuade nonvoters to use their *franchise*?

ENJOYING MEDIA

Movies to See and Web sites to Explore

California Voter Foundation   calvoter.org
A nonprofit, nonpartisan organization promoting and applying the responsible use of technology to improve the democratic process. Their Web site discusses electronic voting issues and provides free candidate information, maps, and political data.

California Fair Political Practices Commission http://www.fppc.ca.gov
The state agency that monitors campaign contributions for all elections in California.

Register to Vote online   sos.ca.gov/elections/elections_
                                       vr.htm
California Secretary of State's official Voter Registration page. You can register to vote online.

Ballotpedia   Ballotpedia.org
Web site with information about ballot measures across the nation.

Bobby, Emilio Estevez, 2006
A fictional account of the people and events at the Ambassador Hotel the day Robert F. Kennedy was assassinated after winning the California presidential primary in 1968. Illustrates the range of people living and

working in Los Angeles in the tumultuous sixties as well as presenting the ideals that Robert F. Kennedy offered to America.

The Candidate, Michael Ritchie, 1972
California in the early 1970s is the backdrop for the story of an idealistic lawyer who runs for U.S. Senate and faces the truth about his integrity in this Oscar-winning film. Over 30 years later, you can watch this and decide if the corruption and moral dilemmas faced by the candidate still exist for today's politicians.

ENDNOTES

1. Gautam Dutta, "Runaway, Budget Busting Runoffs," California Progress Report, April 1, 2009. http://www.newamerica.net/publications/articles/2009/runaway_budget_busting_runoffs_12283.
2. All Mail Election Heads to Final Stretch—Redondo Beach, March 2, 2011. http://www.easyreadernews.com/21217/all-mail-election-heads-to-final-stretch/.
3. Interview with Pat Bradford of Bradford and Rix, August 15, 2003.
4. U.S. Census Bureau, http://quickfacts.census.gov/qfd/states/06000.html.
5. Richard Zeiger, quoting Mervin Field, "Few Citizens Make Decisions for Everyone," *California Journal*, Vol. 21, November 1990, p. 519.
6. "State's Race-Conscious Redistricting in 1990s Sparked Increase in Minority Political Participation," Public Policy Institute of California, Press Release, June 13, 2001. http://www.ppic.org/main/pressrelease.asp?i=303.

CHAPTER EIGHT

The California Legislature

> I came up here to be a legislator, which I thought was like
> being an intellectual in action. What I found was I was an
> assembly worker in a bill factory.
>
> —Tom Hayden, Former Senator (D, Santa Monica)

The California legislative branch is a bicameral body consisting of a
40-member Senate elected for a four-year term and an 80-member
Assembly elected for a two-year term. Half of the Senate and the entire
Assembly are elected in November of even-numbered years.

Each Senate district must be equal in population to all other Senate
districts, with the same rule holding for all Assembly districts. Thus,
each Senate district includes twice as many residents as each Assembly
district, and state senators are considered more powerful than Assembly
members. District boundaries are drawn by the California Citizens'
Commission on Redistricting and are supposed to reflect "communities
of interest," as well as respecting the federal Voting Rights Act
protections for minority groups (see Figure 8.1). There are roughly
931,000 Californians in each State Senate district and about 466,000 in
each Assembly district.

THE STATE OF THE LEGISLATURE:
CHAOS IN MOTION?

Like many political bodies in the United States, California's legislature
often ranks low in public support. While overt corruption (such as
taking campaign contributions in direct exchange for a specific vote) is
rarely discovered or publicized, partisan battles and resulting inaction
can destroy public confidence. Due to the scope and complexity of
their tasks, California's legislators have one of the nation's best pay
and benefit packages, with salaries of over $95,000 per year (higher for
officers of each house) plus generous expense accounts. However, due to

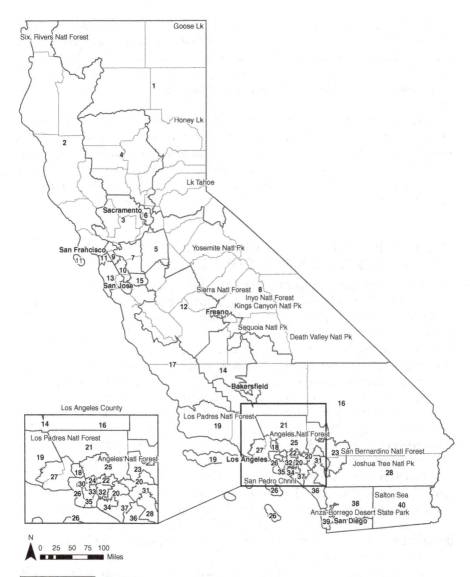

FIGURE 8.1 **California State Senate Districts**

Source: We Draw the Lines, Citizens Redistricting Commission, 2011.

Proposition 140 (1990), legislators can only serve for a limited time and no longer are eligible for any state-funded pension plan.[1]

Term limits have had numerous unexpected consequences. Along with the six-year (three-term) limit on Assembly service and the eight-year (two-term) limit on senators, Proposition 140 also cut legislative budgets in ways that led to the loss of many highly skilled legislative staff members. Rapid turnover in elected legislators and the relative inexperience of their staff members actually gives more power to the over 1,000 registered Sacramento lobbyists,[2] who use their unlimited years of experience to influence the rookie legislators. Nor have term limits ended political ambition: Many legislators now recycle themselves by running for local offices or seeking appointed positions after they are termed out.

Despite all these shortcomings, Proposition 140 has brought new faces to Sacramento and has increased the ethnic and occupational diversity of our legislature. Voters have also been offered ballot propositions to change the term limits so that legislators may serve a total of 12 years in either house, with the idea that longer terms provide more continuity of political experience.

REDISTRICTING AND GERRYMANDERING: WILL THE NEW SYSTEM MAKE A DIFFERENCE?

Because legislators run from specific, numbered districts (80 Assembly and 40 state Senate), voter registration numbers in each district essentially determine which party will hold the legislative seat. District boundaries are redrawn every ten years (after each U.S. Census), in a process known as *redistricting*. For many decades, lines for the state Assembly and Senate were decided by the legislators themselves, which involved a manipulation of the boundaries (known as *gerrymandering*) to protect the majority party's continued dominance. However, voters frustrated with the partisan dynamics of the process passed Proposition 11 (2008), which creates an independent citizen commission to redistrict the legislative boundaries for the 2012 elections, followed by another proposition that gave the Citizens' Commission on Redistricting the authority to draw lines for California's 53 Congressional districts. The Commission's first boundaries produced protests from the California Republican Party as well as from some ethnic organizations, and talk of referendums and lawsuits could derail the Citizens' Commission redistricting efforts and throw the line-drawing into the courts.

Another change for California voters involves Proposition 14 (2010). Now both congressional and legislative races involve "top-two" (also known as voter-nominated) primaries in June with the general election the following November of even-numbered years. The June primaries, unlike the old partisan primary system, provide all voters with the same list of candidates to choose from. Under the new rules, candidates may choose not to mention their party affiliation on the ballot, presumably in an effort to gain the votes of the many nonaffiliated voters. In both June and November elections, voters could see fewer party labels to guide them as they choose their candidates.

COMPARED TO CALIFORNIA

FULL-TIME AND PART-TIME LEGISLATURES IN SELECTED STATES

Full Time: California, Michigan, New York, and Pennsylvania (average pay: $68,599) (California legislators earn $95,291 per year)

Part Time: Montana, New Hampshire, North Dakota, Utah, and Wyoming (average pay: $15,984)

Source: National Conference of State Legislatures Backgrounder, January 2007, http://www.ncsl.org/programs/press/2004/backgrounder_fullandpart.htm

Think Critically: Should elected officials serve part time and thus be involved in the nonpolitical world in order to earn a living? Or do we need their full-time energy and attention?

LEGISLATIVE FUNCTIONS AND PROCEDURES: HOW THEY DO THEIR BUSINESS

Unlike the U.S. Congress, which has complete legislative power in the national government, the California legislature must share lawmaking authority with the voters through the initiative and referendum processes described earlier. However, most state laws are developed by lawmakers in Sacramento. In addition, the legislature has the "power of the purse," levying taxes and appropriating money to finance the operation of all state agencies. After passage of Proposition 13 in June 1978, the legislature also became responsible for providing a large percentage of local government resources.

The legislature meets in two-year sessions. A bill introduced during the first year may continue to be considered during the second year without being reintroduced. When a bill is introduced, it moves slowly (with rare exceptions) through a complex process of committee hearings until it reaches the floor of the house where it began. Every bill must go through at least one committee, pass the full house, move through the second house's committee and floor, and then, finally, be sent to the governor. During this process, most bills are *amended*, in part owing to the extensive lobbying by special interests affected by the legislation's intent.

The powers of the Senate and Assembly are nearly identical, although only the approval of the Senate is needed to confirm certain administrative appointments by the governor. A member of either house can introduce any bill, and a majority of the entire membership of both houses is needed to pass most legislation. Figure 8.2 shows the procedure followed when a bill is introduced. A two-thirds majority is required for

Initial Steps by Author   **Action in House of Origin**

Idea
Suggestions for legislation come from citizens, lobbyists, legislators, businesses, governor, and other public or private agencies.

Drafting
Formal copy of bill and brief summary are prepared by the legislative counsel.

Introduction
Bill is submitted by senator or Assembly member, numbered and read for the first time; Rules Committee assigns bill to a committee. Printed. Action in house of origin.

Committee
Once in committee, testimony is taken from author, proponents, and opponents. Bills can be passed, amended, held (killed), referred to another committee, or sent to interim study. Bills with a fiscal impact are referred to Appropriations Committee (Senate) and Ways and Means (Assembly).

Second Reading
Bills that pass out of committee are read a second time and placed on file for debate.

Floor Debate and Vote
Bills are read a third time and debated. A rollcall vote follows. For ordinary bills, a majority is needed to pass. For urgency bills and appropriation measures, a two-thirds majority is needed. Any member may seek reconsideration and another vote. If passed, the bill is sent to the second house.

FIGURE 8.2 **How a Bill Becomes Law in California**
Source: Los Angeles County Almanac, 1991.

budget bills, proposed constitutional amendments, *overrides* of a veto, and urgency measures, which, unlike most laws, take effect immediately rather than on January 1 of the following year. Urgency measures, unlike regular laws, cannot be overturned by public referendums.

PRESIDING OFFICERS: EACH PARTY GETS SOMETHING

The lieutenant governor is the presiding officer, or president, of the Senate. In that capacity, however, he or she has little power and can vote only in cases of a tie. The person with greatest influence in the Senate is usually the *president pro tem* (for a time), a senator who is elected as a substitute presiding officer by the entire Senate and automatically becomes the chair of the powerful Senate Rules Committee. The pro tem is almost always

Disposition in Second House

Reading
Bill is read for the first time and referred to a committee by the Assembly or Senate Rules Committee.

Committee
Procedures and possible actions are identical to those in the first house.

Second Reading
If approved, the bill is read a second time and placed on the daily file for debate and vote.

Floor Debate and Vote
As in the house of origin, recorded votes are taken after debate. If the bill is passed without having been further amended, it is sent to the governor's desk. (Resolutions are sent to the secretary of state.) If amended in the second house and passed, the measure returns to the house of origin for consideration of amendments.

Resolution of Two-House Differences

Concurrence
The house of origin decides whether to accept the other house's amendments. If approved, the bill is sent to the governor. If rejected, the bill is placed in the hands of a conference committee composed of three senators and three Assembly members.

Conference
If the conferees fail to agree, the bill dies. If the conferees present a recommendation for compromise (called a conference report), both houses vote on the report. If the report is adopted by both, the bill goes to the governor. If either house rejects the report, a second conference committee can be formed.

Role of the Governor

Sign or Veto?
Within 12 days after receiving a bill, the governor can sign it into law, allow it to become law without his signature, or veto it. A vetoed bill returns to the house of origin for possible vote on overriding the veto (requires a two-thirds majority of both houses). Urgency measures become effective immediately after signing. Others usually take effect the following January 1st.

FIGURE 8.2 (continued)

a member of the party with a majority of senators (Democrats have held a majority for over 40 years). To counterbalance the pro tem's power, the minority caucus selects a minority leader to organize its work.

Like the Senate president pro tem, the *speaker of the Assembly* is elected by the entire body and is typically a member of the majority party (with the exception of 1995–1996, Democrats have held a majority for over 40 years). The speaker is supposed to preside over the assembly but often delegates the actual task to a speaker pro tem while the speaker "works the floor" (walks around lobbying the members). The Speaker's approach to governing the legislature could include punitive measures for legislators who do not vote with the majority caucus; in 2011, Assembly member Anthony Portantino (D,Pasadena) refused to vote for the state budget and subsequently was told his entire staff would be suspended from duty.[3] The minority party caucus elects its own floor leader as well as caucus chair.

COMMITTEES: WHERE THE REAL WORK GETS DONE

As in Congress, all members of the legislature serve on at least one *standing committee*. Most members of the Assembly serve on three committees, and most senators on four or five. (Table 8.1 lists standing committees of the state Senate.) Each bill that is introduced is referred to the appropriate

TABLE 8.1

State Senate Standing Committees, 2010–2012

Agriculture
Appropriations
Banking and Financial Institutions
Budget and Fiscal Review
Business, Professions, and Economic Development
Education
Elections and Constitutional Amendments
Energy, Utilities, and Communications
Environmental Quality
Governance and Finance
Governmental Organization
Health
Human Services
Insurance
Judiciary
Labor and Industrial Relations
Legislative Ethics
Natural Resources and Water
Public Employment and Retirement
Public Safety
Rules
Transportation and Housing
Veterans Affairs

Source: California State Senate.

committee and is considered by it in an order usually determined by the chairperson. Most bills that fail to become law are killed in committee; those enacted have often been amended there before being considered on the floor of the Senate or Assembly, where they may be further amended.

In contrast to the situation in the U.S. Congress, committee chairs in the state legislature are not determined by seniority. In the Senate, the power to organize committees and appoint their chairs and members is vested in the Rules Committee, made up of the president pro tem and four other senators (two from each caucus). In addition to the Rules Committee, among the most important are the Education, Budget and Fiscal Review, Banking and Financial Institutions, Transportation and Housing, and Health committees.

In the Assembly, the speaker assigns most committees except for the Rules Committee. Among the most powerful is the Appropriations Committee, which, like the Senate Budget and Fiscal Review Committee, considers all bills that involve state spending. Other important Assembly committees are the Insurance, Education, Agriculture, and Banking and Finance committees.

If either house adds an amendment to a bill that is unacceptable to the house that first passed it, a *conference committee* consisting of three senators and three Assembly members attempts to reach a compromise

DEBATING THE ISSUES

LEGISLATIVE REFORM: HOW MANY VOTES TO INCREASE TAXES?

Viewpoint: The legislature should require only a majority vote to create or continue taxes.

- Majority rules should involve a true majority (50 percent plus one vote).
- The current two-thirds requirement for imposing taxes creates a tyranny of the minority, in which a handful of people can cause severe cuts in state services.

Viewpoint: The current two-thirds requirement to pass new taxes is a good way to ensure caution with public funds.

- The two-thirds requirement for taxes is the only way that the minority party in the legislature has any ability to influence state policy.
- The two-thirds requirement for new taxes insures that the majority party doesn't control state spending.

Ask Yourself: Under what circumstances does a super-majority make sense? Should taxation for California require that level of support in the legislature?

acceptable to both houses. When a bill is finally passed in the same form by both houses, it is sent to the governor for final action.

LOYALTIES IN THE LEGISLATURE: PARTY, PUBLIC, OR PERSONAL?

Does the state legislature serve itself, the parties, or the public? In terms of public services, a critical issue is the state of the economy. During prosperous times when people are employed and spending money, tax revenues are high, and legislators can decide how to spend state money with reasonable amicability. Both parties can look good to their constituents when money flows well. When the state is in recession, bitter battles erupt between the two parties about how to provide services without adequate funds. On nonbudget matters, such as gay marriage or driving laws for minors, political philosophy and lobbying input will influence lawmakers' decisions. Personal style and political experience also have

TABLE 8.2

Recent Laws Created by Our State Legislature and Signed by the Governor: (These are just a few of the 725 laws passed in 2010 that went into effect January 1, 2011.)

- AB 119 (Jones, D-Sacramento) prevents insurance companies from charging different rates for men and women for identical coverage.
- SB 782 (Yee, D-San Francisco) prevents landlords from evicting tenants who are victims of domestic or sexual abuse or stalking.
- AB 1844 (Fletcher, R-San Diego), informally known as Chelsea's Law, will increase penalties, parole provisions, and oversight of sex offenders, including a "one-strike, life-without-parole penalty" for some.
- AB 1871 (Jones, D-Sacramento) allows people to lease out their cars when they are not being used without having to purchase additional automobile insurance.
- AB 537 (Arambula, D-Fresno) will make food stamps an acceptable form of payment at farmers' markets through an Electronic Benefit Transfer (EBT) process.
- SB 1411 (Simitian, D-San Mateo) makes it a misdemeanor to maliciously impersonate someone via a social media outlet or through e-mails.
- SB 1317 (Leno, D-San Francisco) allows the state to fine parents with a $2,000 penalty if their K–8 child misses more than 10 percent of the school year without a valid excuse. It also allows the state to punish parents with up to a year in prison for the misdemeanor.

some impact. Due to term limits, legislators and their leaders rotate out quickly, and many inexperienced lawmakers flounder in attempting to make laws and pass a budget. Public opinion polls consistently show low confidence in lawmakers,[4] and suggestions for change in the legislature continue to be promoted by a variety of interest groups.

Given the many inexperienced legislators and the partisan battles they engage in, the number of bills passed and signed by the governor has declined over recent years. In 2010, only 725 bills were passed and signed, with each one costing approximately a half-million dollars in legislative time and staff.[5] While those who prefer less government may like the idea of fewer new laws, others worry that legislative inaction will result in harm to Californians. See Table 8.2 for recent laws passed by the state legislature and now in effect in California.

QUESTIONS TO CONSIDER

Using Your Text and Your Own Experiences

1. Define *redistricting* and *gerrymandering*. How do the two concepts relate? Has the work of the Citizens Commission on Redistricting reduced gerrymandering? Why or why not?

2. What is your impression of California's legislative system? Is it efficient? Is it responsive to the public? How could the legislative process be improved?

3. How have term limits affected California's lawmaking process? Why do most lawmakers oppose term limits? What do you think of term limits? Should they be revised?

ENJOYING MEDIA

Movies to See and Web sites to Explore

California State Senate   http://www.senate.ca.gov
The 40-member State Senate is the upper house of our legislature.

California State Assembly   http://www.assembly.ca.gov
There are 80 Assembly members elected to represent us.

Legislative Analyst (nonpartisan   lao.ca.gov fiscal & policy
advisor)
The LAO provides serious analysis of legislation and budget issues for the legislative branch.

Capitol Track   capitoltrack.com
Follow legislation online.

Citizens Redistricting Commission   wedrawthelines.ca.gov
Learn how political district boundaries are developed.

Enron: The Smartest Guys in the Room, Alex Gibney, 2005
A multidimensional study of one of the biggest business scandals in American history. Enron executives stole billions and their actions contributed to California's energy crisis of the early 2000s (a problem that became part of the recall campaign against Gray Davis).

ENDNOTES

1. Interview with Mike Ward, Budget Officer of the California State Senate, August 8, 2000.
2. Jamie Court, "Sacramento Scandal-in-Waiting," *Los Angeles Times*, January 24, 2006, p. B13.
3. Interview with Assembly member Anthony Portantino, August 7, 2011.
4. "Time Trends for Job Approval Ratings, Legislature," Statewide Survey, Public Policy Institute of California, July 29, 2009. http://www.ppic.org/main/dataSet.asp?i=927.
5. Dan Walters, "California Capitol's 2009 Prospects Look Grim," *Sacramento Bee*, January 5, 2009.

CHAPTER NINE

California's Plural Executive: Governor Plus Seven

> California governors have been predominantly white men born outside of the state. Only seven governors throughout California's history were California natives, while 29 were born in other states, and two were foreign-born.... Californians have yet to elect a woman, an African American, or an Asian American as governor. The state has had one Hispanic governor, Romualdo Pacheco, Jr., in 1875.
>
> —Just the Facts, Public Policy Institute of California

California's governor is one of the most powerful people in the nation, with powers including spearheading the annual budget process, appointing numerous executive and judicial officers, signing or vetoing legislation, deciding clemency for convicted criminals, and many ceremonial activities.

VETO, BUDGET, AND APPOINTMENTS: THE KEY POWERS

When the legislature passes a bill, the governor has 12 days in which to *veto* it by sending it back to the legislature or to sign it into law. If he or she does neither, the bill becomes law automatically. The only time a governor gets more time is when the legislature goes into recess or adjourns and hundreds of bills may arrive in a few days. In this situation, the governor has 30 days to make decisions about bills. Governors vary in their eagerness to veto, and the frequency of the veto depends in part on whether the governor and the legislative majority are from the same party. If the legislative majority is from the other party, the governor may be sent many bills that are sure to be vetoed because of partisan

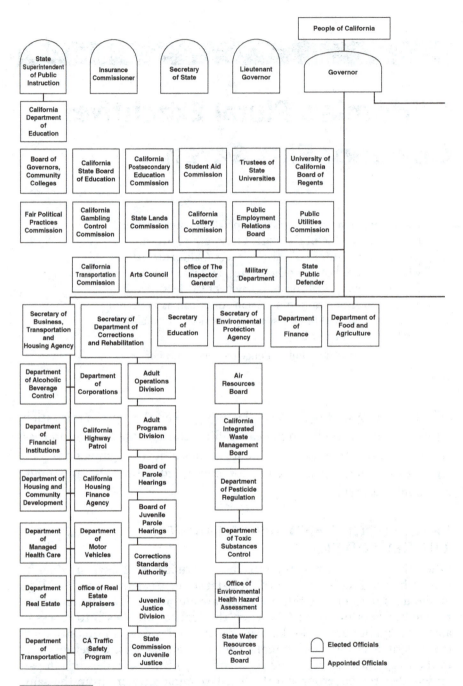

FIGURE 9.1 **California State Government: The Executive Branch**

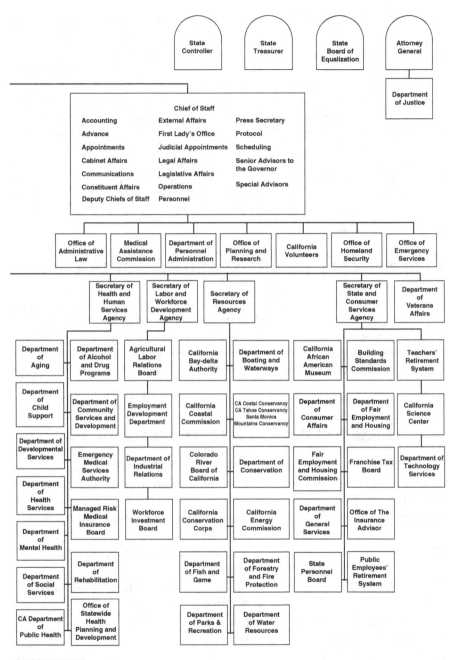

FIGURE 9.1 (continued)

conflicts or ideological differences. Only rarely can the legislature amass the two-thirds vote necessary to *override* a veto, so the governor's veto is a very powerful tool.

The budget powers begin with a ceremonial moment: Every January 10th, the governor presents a budget proposal to the legislature for the fiscal year starting July 1st. Although the bill may be much amended before it is passed and returned to the governor in June, he or she may then use the *item veto*. This permits the deletion of a particular expenditure entirely or the reduction of its amount, thereby giving the governor major control over state spending, from start to finish. Appointment powers include giving positions both in the judicial branch and in the executive bureaucracy (see Figure 9.1). The individuals who are appointed to these high-level positions can shape the effectiveness of our courts as well as numerous state agencies.

OTHER POWERS: NEW IDEAS AND "LIFE OR DEATH" CHOICES

The governor's other powers include various "checks and balances" with the legislative and judicial branches (Table 9.1). For the legislature, the governor's powers include sending messages to suggest new legislation and the authority to call special sessions. Ideas for new laws are often announced in the annual State of the State speech, which is usually given along with

TABLE 9.1

Checks and Balances: The Governor's Appointments

Vacant Position	Who Must Confirm Governor's Nominee
Judicial: Appeals courts and state Supreme Court	Commission on Judicial Appointments
Judicial: Superior courts	No one (valid until next scheduled election)
U.S. Senate	No one (valid until next scheduled election)
County supervisor	No one (valid until next scheduled election)
Governor's personal staff	No one
Governor's cabinet	State Senate
Executive departments	State Senate
Boards and commissions	State Senate
Constitutional officers	State Senate and Assembly
Board of Equalization	State Senate and Assembly

DEBATING THE ISSUES

THE GOVERNOR'S POWERS

Viewpoint: The governor has too much power over the state budget, the judicial branch, and the administrative departments. Powers should be redistributed to the legislature or the voters.

- There is no adequate oversight of **gubernatorial** decisions about judicial appointments.
- The legislature should be required to approve more of the governor's appointees.

Viewpoint: The governor needs all the current powers granted in the state constitution and should retain them.

- The governor is elected to use judgment and make decisions without constant interference by others.
- The governor is adequately balanced by the people's direct democracy powers—they can even recall the governor.

Ask Yourself: What issues are within the governor's power? Do people know all the aspects of executive power when they vote for governor?

the budget proposal. Concepts presented here can then be introduced as bills into the state Assembly or Senate by the governor's allies in those bodies. In addition, the governor can call a special election, regardless of any opposition to this costly action.

Perhaps the governor's most emotionally difficult power is *executive clemency*, which consists of pardons, commutations (reductions of sentences), and reprieves (postponements of sentences) granted to convicts. Governors may grant a life sentence instead of execution to those already handed a death sentence by a jury and court, but such actions rarely occur.

UNUSUAL CIRCUMSTANCES: MILITARY AND POLICE POWERS

The governor, as commander-in-chief of the California National Guard, may call the guard into active duty for in-state emergencies. Because the National Guard can also be called to duty by the president for national service, many California National Guard members have also served in foreign interventions. The governor may also direct the California Highway Patrol to bolster local police and sheriff's officers if action is needed on a smaller scale. Generally, governors hope that California remains free of earthquakes, floods, major fires, or riots during their term of office, thus avoiding any need to use these powers.

APPOINTMENT POWERS: JOBS AT THE TOP

The governor enforces state laws through a vast administrative bureaucracy consisting of about 50 departments, most of which are currently grouped within five huge agencies: Business, Transportation and Housing, Health and Welfare Resources, State and Consumer Services, and Youth and Adult Corrections (see Figure 9.1). The heads of these agencies, in addition to the directors of the Departments of Finance, Food and Agriculture, Industrial Relations, Trade and Commerce, Environmental Protection, Child Development and Education, and the Director of Information Technology, constitute the governor's cabinet and are appointed by the governor, subject to Senate confirmation. The finance director is responsible for preparing the entire state budget for submission to the legislature. In keeping with California's tradition of mistrust of political patronage, the governor actually appoints only 1 percent of the total state workforce, with the remaining state employees being unionized civil servants.[1] However, those several hundred appointed jobs are at the highest levels of government and determine the functioning of virtually every state-run operation.

The governor also has the power to appoint members of dozens of administrative boards, four of which are in the field of education. Most appointments are made with the concurrence of the state Senate, and appointees are usually political supporters of the governor, including termed-out legislators. Many of the board appointees are uncompensated except for a minimal per diem and expenses of attending meetings, while others earn salaries that some consider excessive, given the workload. Among these are the following:

1. The Board of Regents, which governs the nine campuses of the University of California (UC) and consists of 18 members appointed by the governor for 12-year terms, seven ex-officio members, and one UC student who serves a one-year term. Compensation: $100 per meeting day.

2. The Board of Trustees of the 20-campus California State University system, composed of 18 gubernatorial appointees who serve eight-year terms and five ex-officio members. Compensation: $100 per meeting day.

3. The Board of Governors of the California Community Colleges, a 16-member group (including one faculty and one student member) appointed by the governor for four-year terms to coordinate the 72 locally controlled community college districts. Compensation: $100 per meeting day.

4. The State Board of Education, with 11 members appointed for four-year terms to make policy for public schools throughout the state on such matters as curriculum and textbook selection. Compensation: $100 per meeting day.

5. The nine-member High Speed Rail Authority, of whom the governor appoints five, which helps plan for an 800-mile high-speed rail system to connect all major California cities. Compensation: $100 per meeting day.

6. The five-person Public Utilities Commission, appointed for six-year terms, which regulates the rates charged and services provided in the gas, water, telephone, telegraph, electricity, and transportation industries. Compensation: $127,000 annually.

7. The five-member Energy Commission, appointed for five-year terms for the purpose of coordinating energy needs and resources as well as promoting conservation and alternative technologies. Compensation: $117,000 annually.

8. The seven-member Fair Employment and Housing Commission, with four-year terms and responsibility for enforcing the laws against both job and housing discrimination. Compensation: $100 per meeting day.

9. The Unemployment Insurance Appeals Board, with the governor appointing four of seven members, which reviews appeals regarding unemployment and disability claims. Compensation: $123,987 annually.

10. The Board of Parole Hearings, with 17 members who determine which convicts should be granted parole from state prisons. Compensation: $99,693 annually.

11. The five-member Agricultural Labor Relations Board, which guarantees justice for California agricultural workers and stability in agricultural labor relations. Compensation: $127,833 annually.

12. Four of the 12 members of the California Coastal Commission, authorized to protect the coastline for public access. Compensation: $100 per meeting day.

Most governors try to balance political patronage with some semblance of screening for qualifications before they appoint their supporters to government positions. Because most appointments require state Senate approval, the governor's relationship with the majority party in the Senate may determine whether or not appointees are confirmed. The Senate has been known to be very selective, withholding approval of the governor's first choice if the majority party is unhappy with the governor's policies, or if the Senate leaders consider the nominee to be underqualified.

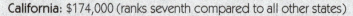

COMPARED TO CALIFORNIA

GOVERNOR SALARIES FROM SELECTED STATES

California: $174,000 (ranks seventh compared to all other states)

New York: $179,000 (highest)

Arizona: $95,000

Maine: $70,000 (lowest)

Source: Andrew Knapp, "Govs' salaries range," Special to Stateline.org, May 15, 2007, http://www.stateline.org/live/details/story?contentId=207914

Think Critically: Should a state governor earn more than 95 percent of the people? Or should the governor earn the same as the average Californian? What are the arguments for and against high salaries for elected leaders?

In addition to the many state boards and commissions the governor must fill, he or she also has the authority to appoint replacements to fill vacancies created by death or resignation on county boards of supervisors as well as those occurring for any of the seven other executive officers and for California's U.S. senators. With so many responsibilities, California's governor is certainly comparable in importance to top corporate executives, yet the governor's salary is $174,000 per year, much less than the multimillion-dollar salaries of most corporate leaders. As an independently wealthy individual, Governor Arnold Schwarzenegger chose to take a symbolic $1 per year; however, most governors have not had the personal luxury of turning down the salary.

THE PLURAL EXECUTIVE: TRAINING FOR FUTURE GOVERNORS

In addition to the governor, seven other executive officials are elected directly by the voters. Like the governor, they are chosen for four-year terms (with a limit of two terms) and hold the following positions, often known as *constitutional offices.*

1. The lieutenant governor, in addition to being nominal president of the state Senate, succeeds to the governorship if that office becomes vacant between elections. The lieutenant governor also serves as acting governor when the governor is out of the state. A recall of the governor does not create a vacancy; the process actually includes the selection of a replacement governor, and the office of lieutenant governor is not affected. Because of the *office-block ballot,* with its emphasis on voting separately for each state office, Californians have

often elected a governor from one party and a lieutenant governor from the other party. This system, in which the second in command may be from a different party than the governor, has been criticized for promoting inefficiency and poor coordination between public officials. Democrat Gavin Newsom from San Francisco is the current lieutenant governor.

2. The attorney general, the chief legal adviser to all state agencies, is also head of the state Justice Department, which provides assistance to local law enforcement agencies, represents the state in lawsuits, and exercises supervision over the county district attorneys in their prosecution of state criminal defendants. Democrat Kamala Harris (San Francisco) is the first woman and first African American to serve as attorney general.

3. The controller is concerned with government finance. He or she audits state expenditures, supervises financial restrictions on local governments, and influences state tax collections as a member of the Board of Equalization. Moreover, the controller has considerable patronage power in appointing inheritance tax appraisers and is a member of the State Lands Commission, which oversees the state's 4 million acres of public lands. He or she is also chair of the Franchise Tax Board, which collects income taxes. Democrat John Chiang serves as controller and is widely known for his decision to enforce Proposition 25 (2010) by deciding to withhold legislative salaries if the legislature missed the state budget deadline in June 2011. (They met their deadline.)

4. The California secretary of state maintains official custody over state legal documents, grants charters to business corporations, and administers state election procedures. One of the most important tasks of the secretary of state is to verify the signatures on petitions for ballot initiatives, referendums, and recalls, and to administer state election laws. Democrat Debra Bowen, former assembly member and state senator, will be termed out in 2014.

5. The state treasurer maintains custody over tax money collected by various state agencies, deposits it in private banks until appropriated by the legislature, sells government bonds (presumably at the lowest possible interest rate), and influences stock investments by the public-employee pension funds. Democrat Bill Lockyer, who has served in numerous positions in California government, will term out in 2014.

6. Until 1988, the insurance commissioner was appointed by the governor. A ballot initiative made the position an elected post. The insurance commissioner's job is to monitor the corporations that sell various types of insurance: life, health, automobile, homeowner, earthquake, and any other forms of insurance sold in the state. Democrat Dave Jones was elected to this office in 2010.

7. The superintendent of public instruction is designated by the state constitution to be elected on a nonpartisan basis in the hopes that education policy will remain nonpartisan. The superintendent directs the state Department of Education and is charged with the responsibility for dispensing financial aid to local school districts, granting teaching credentials, and enforcing policies determined by the state Board of Education. In addition, the superintendent is an *ex-officio* member of the UC Board of Regents and the California State University Board of Trustees. Democrat Tom Torlakson won this office in 2010 with strong support from teacher unions.

In addition to the constitutional executive officers just mentioned, California voters choose four members of the Board of Equalization from the four districts into which the state is divided for this purpose. This board, the nation's only elected tax commission, collects the state sales tax as well as assisting the 58 county assessors to collect correct property taxes. The four elected members currently include two Asian American women and one African American.

The California executive branch also includes numerous agencies (see Figure 9.1) whose thousands of state employees are the individuals who provide direct services to Californians at the Department of Motor Vehicles, the Employment Development Department, the Department of Health Services, and many more agencies. Due to state budget cuts, many of these agencies now provide services on a reduced basis, often causing delays and aggravation for Californians seeking assistance.

Numerous efforts to study the state's bureaucracy and reduce duplication or waste have resulted in little change. Although the state appears top-heavy with agencies, boards, and commissions, when brought into scrutiny, the workload and purpose of each one seems to be justified. Keeping professionals licensed and reviewed (Board of Registered Nursing, Dental Board, Engineers and Land Surveyors, and dozens more); maintaining standards for human safety (California Environmental Protection Agency, Building Standards Commission, Seismic Safety Commission, Labor Standards Enforcement, and more); and protecting consumers (Pesticide Regulation, Food and Agriculture, Office of Privacy Protection, and more) all serve to keep California a safer, healthier place to live.

QUESTIONS TO CONSIDER

Using Your Text and Your Own Experiences

1. Describe some of the governor's powers. Which ones are most important (i.e., affect large numbers of people and are used frequently)? Which ones does a governor prefer not to use?

2. Discuss the governor's powers to appoint government officials. How does this power help shape the everyday lives of Californians? Give specific examples.

3. What is the relationship between the governor and the legislature? What checks and balances are built into the California constitution for these two branches of government?

ENJOYING MEDIA

Movies to See and Web sites to Explore

Governor's Home Page   gov.ca.gov
See all the latest news from the Governor.

California Secretary of State   ss.ca.gov
Secretary of State Web site includes voter registration information, campaign finance disclosures, and more.

Governor Jerry Brown's Index   http://gov.ca.gov/docs/
of Appointed Positions   Statutory-Index-2011.pdf

Schwarzenegger: I'll Be Back, Birgit Kienzle, 2007
A German filmmaker interviews Californians to figure out how the body builder-actor became California's governor and navigated his way through his first term to be reelected in 2006.

ENDNOTE

1. Bradley Inman, "Many Are Calling But Few Will Be Chosen," *Los Angeles Times*, March 17, 1991, p. D2.

CHAPTER TEN

Paying the Bills: California's Budget Struggles

> To compete in the world economy, we need to be investing.
> But investing takes money. If we postpone the investments,
> we postpone the benefits and make California a less
> competitive place to work and live.
>
> —Steven Levy, Center for the Continuing Study of the California Economy

Perhaps the most persistent problem of all governments is finding adequate financial resources to do the many tasks expected of the public sector. Even as people complain incessantly about insufficient levels of service, many of them also fiercely resist being taxed to pay for needed improvements. Such contradictions become even more acute in difficult economic times when unemployment rises (thus reducing the total amount of income tax paid) and the needs for unemployment funds, educational opportunities, or welfare programs increase. In prosperous periods, tax collections generally rise, and politicians are tempted to offer "tax cuts," even though not all public services are fully funded. Whether the economy is booming or in a slump, government has only a few options: raise somebody's taxes, provide fewer services, or borrow money and pay it back (with interest, of course) in the future. Each of these alternatives has its own consequences and costs, and it is the process of making these decisions that becomes the annual state budget battle.

HOW THE BUDGET IS DEVELOPED:
A TWO-YEAR PROCESS

Every January, the governor must present to the legislature a budget plan reflecting the governor's priorities. This budget requires many months of preparation and input from the executive branch's various departments and agencies, under the supervision of the Department of Finance. The budget is based on "guesstimates" of the amount the state will collect in taxes and *baseline budgets* from each of the state agencies, cities, counties, and special districts that rely on the state as their primary source of funds. Baseline (or rollover) budgets essentially assume that an agency needs to continue doing everything it currently does as well as receive some cost-of-living adjustment (COLA) raise from the previous year's budget. Of course, agencies may also ask for new funds to provide additional programs, and the governor may wish to initiate new services or reorganize existing programs.

The governor's budget then is examined by the nonpartisan legislative analyst, who reviews the governor's expenditure requests and revenue projections and provides each legislator with comments. Then the legislature begins public hearings held before five subcommittees in each house. During these hearings, state and local government employees (along with the people they serve) testify about why their particular *appropriations* must be maintained or perhaps expanded. Lobbyists for business interests also register their concerns about any taxation changes that may negatively affect their industries.

It is during these budget hearings that the day dreaded by many Californians arrives: April 15. Once tax day is over, the director of finance knows more clearly how much the state has received in personal income taxes and can reevaluate earlier revenue projections to determine whether or not the original budget is accurate. Based on these revised numbers, the governor submits the "May revise." The legislature again discusses the budget, and a conference committee is formed to develop a joint Senate and Assembly budget plan. An additional layer of discussion occurs among the "Big Five," the governor and the two top leaders of each house of the legislature.

By June 15, both houses of the legislature must pass the budget by a simple majority. However, any tax increase requires a two-thirds majority, and because the Republican caucus ferociously opposes all forms of taxation, the state budget in recent times is primarily a document of cutbacks and program eliminations. Because the 2011–2012 budget did not include enough cuts to satisfy the Republicans, that budget passed with no Republican votes. Meanwhile, the substantial cuts to education and social services resulted in many reluctant Democratic votes. The budget must be signed by the governor by June 30. (See Table 10.1.) Until recently, the legislature required a two-thirds majority to pass the budget, and long delays in getting through the legislature were common. Since the passage of Proposition 25 (2010), the budget needs only a simple majority, and legislators do not receive their paychecks if the budget is late. Perhaps due to the personal financial needs of legislators, post-Proposition 25 budgets have been passed on time.

TABLE 10.1

California Budget Process

Executive Branch		Legislative Branch
Administrative departments prepare budgetary requests.	April	
Agencies prepare preliminary program budgets.	May	
Department of Finance and governor issue policy directions.	July August	
Department of Finance reviews agency proposals.	September October	
Commission on State Finance and experts forecast revenues.	November	
Governor finalizes budget and sends it to the state printing office.	January	
Governor submits budget to legislature.	January 10	Fiscal committee chairs introduce governor's proposal as budget bill.
	February	Legislative analyst studies proposed budget; issues analysis of budget bill and
	March	perspectives and issues.
	April	Assembly and Senate budget subcommittees hold public hearings on assigned sections of the budget.
Department of Finance issues revised forecast of revenues and expenditures.	May	Subcommittees complete action on budget. Full budget committees hold hearings and vote. Assembly and Senate pass respective versions of the budget bill.
	June	Conference committee of three Assembly members and three senators agree on a compromise budget bill.
	June 15	Legislature submits approved budget to governor.
Governor exercises item veto and signs budget act.	June 30–July	Legislature can restore vetoed items by two-thirds vote in each house.

DEBATING THE ISSUES

BORROWING OUR FUTURE

Viewpoint: The state has no choice except to borrow money to build roads, schools, and water systems for the future needs of California.

- There are not enough current revenues to build the necessary infrastructure.
- Roads, schools, water systems, and other infrastructure will benefit people for decades in the future, so they can help pay for those investments.
- Careful borrowing and clear repayment plans are used by all governments.

Viewpoint: The state should stop borrowing and pay "as you go" with current tax revenues.

- We should not burden our children and grandchildren with bond debts.
- We can reorganize our current state budget priorities so there is money for building infrastructure.
- We should live within our means as a state, never borrowing.

Ask Yourself: How do I manage my personal budget? How would I vote if I were a legislator?

Once the budget bill reaches the governor, the chief executive can then utilize the *item veto* to reduce appropriations or even eliminate whole programs. The legislature rarely has the two-thirds majority to override specific item vetoes, leaving the governor in ultimate control over state spending. Even after the budget is completed and signed, lawsuits challenging the budget are often filed. Although the courts may take years to finalize a decision, the budget goes into effect for the time being.

SOURCES OF REVENUE: NEVER ENOUGH

The five major sources of money for the state are:

1. *The general fund,* which includes state income tax, sales taxes, bank and corporation taxes, and interest earned by the state on money not currently in use. Personal income tax and sales tax provide about half

the state's annual revenues. So as long as there is high unemployment, the state will have reduced revenues. This dependence on the unpredictable economy causes California's tax structure to be labeled "volatile."[1]

2. *Special funds*, including motor vehicle license and registration fees, gasoline taxes, and portions of the sales, cigarette, and horse-racing taxes that are earmarked for specified purposes.

3. *Bond funds*, requiring voter approval, which are monies borrowed from investors and returned to them in the future with interest.

4. *Federal funds*, including "free" money and some grants that require matching state or local commitments.

5. *Miscellaneous revenues*, such as community college fees and contributions to state pension plans.

Property taxes are not included because they are collected by the counties to be spent primarily on local government and educational districts. Figures 10.1 and 10.2 show state revenues and expenditures, respectively, and Figure 10.3 indicates funding sources for the state infrastructure.

Controversies over these revenue sources are endless. Which taxes should be raised? Which should be lowered? Business interests want to reduce any taxes that cut into their profits, while individuals almost always seem to feel that they are paying too much. The Republican viewpoint has traditionally insisted on reducing taxes regardless of impacts on programs, while Democrats have often proposed closing

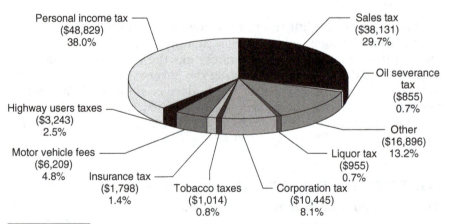

FIGURE 10.1 **State Revenues from Taxes 2009–2010**

Source: Governor's Budget.

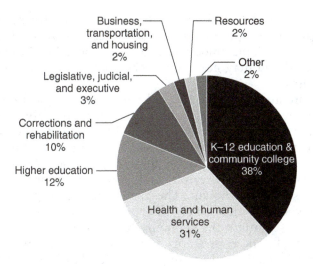

FIGURE 10.2 **General Fund Expenditures by Function, 2008–2009**

Source: Center on Budget and Policy Priorities, "Governor's Budget Summary, 2009–2010," http://www.cbpp.org/cms/?fa=view&id=711

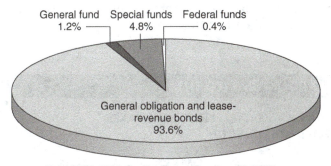

Total 2002–2003 Capital Outlay Funding: $2.2 Billion

FIGURE 10.3 **State Infrastructure Funding Sources (Excluding Transportation)**

Source: Legislative Analysts Office.

loopholes that benefit the wealthy in order to protect low-income residents. One Sacramento budget trick is to create "fees" that are very similar to taxes but can be implemented with only a simple majority, instead of the two-thirds requirement for actual taxes. Another frequent tactic is to "take it to the voters" by putting initiatives on the state ballot to gain voter input for various tax or fee increases. Of course, this approach requires large amounts of campaign spending in order to gain voter approval and may not achieve the goal due to voter rejection of such measures.

Voters are also directly involved when state or local governments borrow money through *bond measures*, which usually require voter approval and are almost always initiated by elected officials in order to build or renovate public facilities. In California, state and local bond funds, with rare exceptions, may only be used for actual capital investments (i.e., construction) and may not be used for ongoing operating costs of government. The historic record suggests that during hard times voters are less likely to approve bonds even though a bond measure may stimulate the economy by creating work for architects, land-use consultants, contractors, construction companies, and so on. All state bonds require only a simple majority, but local bonds now fall into two categories: education bonds (for school districts and community colleges), which require a 55 percent majority, and bonds for other local needs (libraries, police and fire bonds, parks, etc.), which must be passed with a two-thirds vote. Due to the state's fiscal difficulties, California's bond rating (which determines the interest rates that lenders can command when they purchase bonds) has been lowered, and the state and many cities must pay more interest than in the past when they seek lenders to purchase their bonds.

COMPARED TO CALIFORNIA

SALES, GAS, CIGARETTE, AND INCOME TAXES IN SELECTED STATES, 2010

	Sales (%)	Gas per Gallon	Cigarettes per Pack($)	Income (%)
California	8.25	0.46	0.87	1–10
Arizona	6.6	0.19	2.00	2.59–4.54
Oregon	None	0.25	1.18	5–11
Nevada	6.85	0.33	0.80	None

Source: Tax Foundation, Washington, DC, 2010, http://www.taxfoundation.org/news/show/245.html

Think Critically: Do you like California's tax structure as compared with other states? Which taxes would you raise or lower if you had the power?

VOTER DECISIONS AND STATE FINANCE: DEMOCRACY IN ACTION?

In addition to voting on bond measures, voters have utilized ballot initiatives to make fiscal policy for the state. One of the turning points for California's tax policies was Proposition 13 (June 1978), also known as the Jarvis–Gann initiative in recognition of the efforts of landlord Howard Jarvis and his ally Paul Gann to get the initiative on the ballot. Although its passage occurred over 30 years ago, Proposition 13's causes and consequences are still vital elements in understanding California's situation today.

The roots of Proposition 13 lay in the massive national and international *inflation* of the early 1970s. The causes of the inflationary spiral were primarily outside California, including factors such as heavy federal spending in the 1960s and the oil embargo of the early 1970s; nevertheless, these circumstances added to the traditional speculation in land and property in the state and fueled an enormous rise in the real estate values on which property taxes are levied. Homeowners were suddenly confronted with doubled and tripled *tax assessments* from their county assessor. Faced with the risk of losing their homes, middle- and low-income homeowners gladly joined Jarvis and other major property holders in supporting Proposition 13. When public employees claimed that the proposition would cut not only property taxes on which local governments relied heavily but also public services, Jarvis replied that "only the fat" would be cut and that the state budget surplus would rescue counties, cities, and school districts if necessary.

These arguments were extremely persuasive—Proposition 13 passed by a landslide, and all property taxes were limited to 1 percent of the assessed value of the property as of 1976, with reassessment to occur only when the property was sold. Since a budget surplus had accumulated in Sacramento, the state did bail out the local governments for several years, but many services were cut back, including library accessibility, fine arts and athletics in the schools, and parks and recreation. In addition, Proposition 13 had some unforeseen long-term impacts, including the shift from local control to a Sacramento-based funding system for cities, counties, and school districts. There were yet other flaws in the measure: notably property owners who rarely sell (such as commercial property owners) experience almost no increase in taxes, whereas owners of individual homes, which are sold more frequently, confront reassessments up to the current market value, causing dramatic tax increases when a home changes hands. Even two neighboring homeowners in identical homes may pay vastly differing property taxes based on when they purchased their homes. This disparity led the U.S. Supreme Court to refer to Proposition 13 as "distasteful and unwise," even as the Court upheld the legality of the law in a 1991 challenge.

During tight economic times, the state's ability to assist local governments is reduced. State budget cuts force cities, counties, schools, and community college districts to go on frequent "begging" expeditions to Sacramento, and in recent years the combined costs of lobbying Sacramento have made local governments, added together, one of the highest-spending lobbying categories.[2]

Through their ballot activism, voters have also placed tight restrictions on the state budget itself. Proposition 98 (1988) requires the state to spend 40 percent of its annual revenue on K–14 education, while another 15–20 percent of the budget is set aside to finance bond commitments and voter-mandated programs such as prison construction. Another 25–30 percent is mandated by federal law to provide health and welfare assistance, although federal welfare reform does permit the state somewhat more flexibility in how it provides temporary assistance for needy families (TANF).

FUTURE PROSPECTS: THE ENDLESS DEBATE

California and its people have ridden a rollercoaster of economic ups and downs since the end of the Cold War. The early 1990s recession, created mostly by the sudden loss of defense/military jobs, combined with downsizing and mergers in banking and other industries to create a sharp drop in income and sales tax collections. By the mid-1990s, the economy had recovered, especially through the high-tech boom of Silicon Valley's dot-com industry. However, this boom turned into a bust by the year 2000, and the tragedy of September 11, 2001, hurt California's tourism, airlines, and other industries even as the Enron-driven energy crisis ate up billions of dollars. The Great Recession of 2008, with its roots in the housing market and mortgage industry, hit California harder than the rest of the nation, creating a state unemployment rate of more than 12 percent by 2011.[3]

In addition to the domestic policies that create or aggravate recessions, the ongoing unpredictable tides of the global economy, including the impacts of *outsourcing* and *runaway production*, continue to contribute to repeated economic swings. Owing partly to Proposition 13, California relies heavily on volatile income tax revenues, while most states have more property taxes to work with. Public opinion surveys indicate that Californians want lots of public service but are reluctant to be taxed to pay for it.[4] Polls indicate that Californians prefer to cut prisons rather than education or social services, but many prison costs are mandated by the federal government.[5] One often-mentioned source of increased revenues would be a change in Proposition 13 to "split" property tax rolls so that commercial property could be reassessed every ten years and taxed at current value, while maintaining individual homeowners' tax rates for the entire time they own their homes.

During every phase of the state budget cycle, hundreds of groups lobby for their share of revenues while others fight to avoid their share of taxes. Whether or not the economy is strong, everyone wants a piece of the California Dream: schoolchildren and their parents, open-space advocates, prison guards, public employees, library users, college students, welfare (TANF) recipients, automobile users, beachgoers, immigrants, people with disabilities, farmworkers, landowners—the list is endless. For the foreseeable future, California's budget process is bound to be an annual agony that profoundly affects all Californians. Only an informed and politically active public can hope to be considered as elected officials debate the state's budget priorities. Ignoring the process, or the players, may be easy in the short run, but ultimately, we all pay a price if we remain ignorant or uninvolved.

QUESTIONS TO CONSIDER

Using Your Text and Your Own Experiences

1. How does the general economy affect government budgets? What is the role of government in helping the economy grow?
2. Describe the revenue sources and expense patterns of state government. Who benefits from the current structure? Who loses?
3. Evaluate the budget process through its annual cycle. What are some problems with the process? Should anything be changed?

ENJOYING MEDIA

Movies to See and Web sites to Explore

Department of Finance   dof.ca.gov
The most important department when it comes to the governor's budget process; the DOF creates the proposal the governor presents on January 10.

Online CA Budget 2007–2008   ebudget.ca.gov
This Web site allows all Californians to see what the state budget is about.

SICKO, Michael Moore, 2007
California's lawmakers and voters are grappling with health-care issues and how to finance health care in California; Michael Moore shows how other nations handle their people's health-care needs.

The Damnedest, Finest Ruins, James Dalessandro, 2006
Vintage film and the voice of opera star Enrico Caruso tell the story of the 1906 earthquake that destroyed San Francisco and of the politicians who let the city burn. Viewers can decide if political errors still impact how we recover from disasters.

ENDNOTES

1. Tracy Gordon and Margaret Weston, "California Budget: Planning for the Future," Public Policy Institute of California, January 2011. http://www.ppic.org/content/pubs/report/R_111TGR.pdf.
2. Secretary of State, Lobbying Expenditures and the Top 100 Lobbying Firms, April 1–June 30, 1994, issued September 1994.
3. "California Employment Development Department," *News Release*, No. 11–67, August 19, 2011. http://www.edd.ca.gov/About_EDD/pdf/urate201108.pdf.
4. Public Policy Institute of California, Statewide Survey: Californians and their Government, June 1, 2011. http://www.ppic.org/content/pubs/survey/S_511MBS.pdf.
5. Public Policy Institute of California, Californians and Their Government, May 2011. http://www.ppic.org/content/pubs/survey/S_511MBS.pdf.

CHAPTER ELEVEN

California Courts and Judges

Courts are places of last resort, so to cut them is to do great harm to the public.
>   —Tani Cantil-Sakauye, Chief Justice of the California
>   state Supreme Court

Unlike the federal system, in which judges are appointed by the president, confirmed by the U.S. Senate, and serve for life with no further review, California's system involves a complicated combination of appointments and elections for judges. This complex system classifies judges into two categories: trial court judges and appeals judges. The judges and their courts serve the largest population in the nation, cost approximately $3 billion per year to run, and receive nearly two-thirds of that money from the state.[1] Over 2,000 judicial officers and 15,000 employees deal with over 10 million civil and criminal cases per year.[2] Severe budget cuts from Sacramento have created reduced hours and partial closures of courtrooms around the state, with resulting delays in divorce proceedings, custody disputes, and many other civil matters. The state has more attorneys per person than anywhere else in the world, but the high costs of legal services (including attorney fees as well as court filing fees) leave many Californians, both middle and low income, at risk of being left out of the legal system. Californians with possible legal concerns can find suggestions for low-cost legal advice on the Web site http://www.courtinfo.ca.gov/selfhelp/lowcost/lawyers.htm.

Among the many tasks of the court system is its role in evaluating controversial ballot measures passed by voters in order to determine if the proposition conflicts with the state constitution. If well-funded interest groups are concerned about the issue (such as gay marriage), state supreme court rulings are often appealed to the U.S. Supreme Court for further review.

CALIFORNIA'S TRIAL COURTS: THE FIRST ROUND

California's trial courts (also known as superior courts) handle the first round of both civil and criminal cases. Civil matters include all aspects of family law (divorce, custody, adoption), as well as the many varieties of civil litigation (malpractice, personal injury, bankruptcy, etc.). Criminal trials usually involve misdemeanor and felony charges. Many superior court judges have taken pay cuts in recent years in order to protect court budgets[3] and in some counties, they are assisted by court commissioners who can perform many of the judges' functions at a lower pay scale. Courts are organized through counties, with 58 superior court systems ranging from Los Angeles County, which employs hundreds of judges, to Alpine County, with only a few judges. Courts may be specialized to handle traffic-related charges, small (civil) claims, or juvenile cases.

ALTERNATIVES TO THE COURTS: BUYING JUDICIAL SERVICES

Because of the overcrowded and often delayed court system, Californians, sometimes unwillingly, have turned to private judges to resolve their civil differences. Many Californians do not realize that when they accept many job opportunities or join most health insurance plans, they must sign a binding arbitration clause that denies them the right to sue in court and, instead, requires them to go to binding (no-appeals) arbitration to resolve disputes with the employer or insurer. Private arbitration is different from mediation; mediation is used to resolve issues outside of court, but mediation does not include a no-appeals agreement. Private arbitration judges (often retired public judges) who handle binding arbitration cases have been criticized for having excessive power, since their decisions are not appealable. Meanwhile, alternative dispute resolution (ADR) services are encouraged by the courts in order to save tax dollars, leaving the costs of resolving civil matters to the individuals. In some cases, ADR can reduce costs of litigation. However, some have accused the courts of developing a "tollroad" for the affluent to save time and, in cases of high-profile individuals, to avoid the publicity of a public trial.

WHERE APPEAL RIGHTS REMAIN INTACT: COURTS IN ACTION

For those who cannot afford or do not wish to use private alternatives, one advantage of using local trial courts to resolve legal problems is the right to appeal. When an individual believes that a lower court has made a legal error in deciding a case, he or she may appeal—if financial resources are available to do so. California is divided into six court of appeal districts, headquartered in San Francisco, Los Angeles, Sacramento, Fresno, San Jose, and San Diego, with a total of 105 judges (see Figure 11.1).

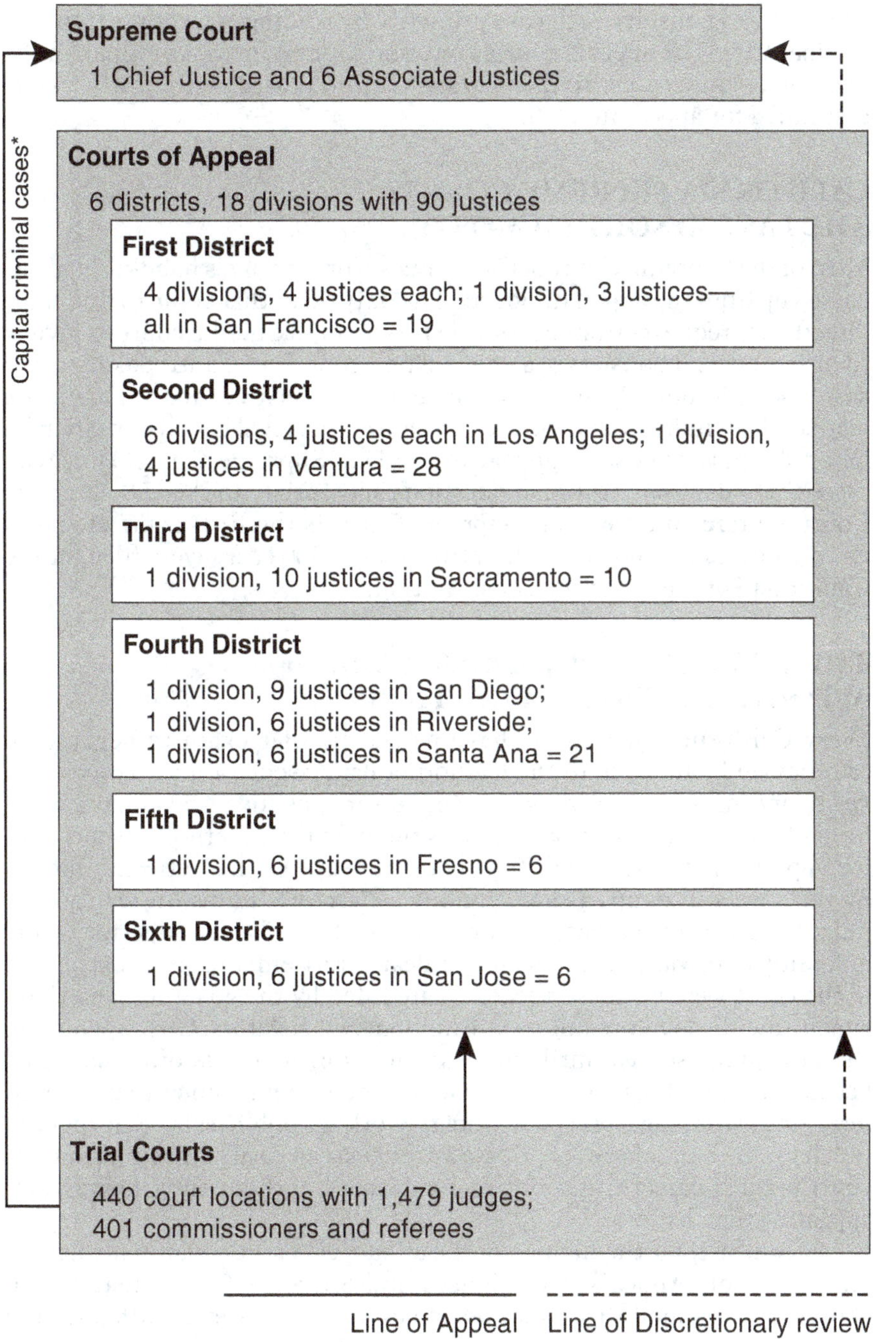

Supreme Court

1 Chief Justice and 6 Associate Justices

Capital criminal cases*

Courts of Appeal

6 districts, 18 divisions with 90 justices

First District

4 divisions, 4 justices each; 1 division, 3 justices—
all in San Francisco = 19

Second District

6 divisions, 4 justices each in Los Angeles; 1 division,
4 justices in Ventura = 28

Third District

1 division, 10 justices in Sacramento = 10

Fourth District

1 division, 9 justices in San Diego;
1 division, 6 justices in Riverside;
1 division, 6 justices in Santa Ana = 21

Fifth District

1 division, 6 justices in Fresno = 6

Sixth District

1 division, 6 justices in San Jose = 6

Trial Courts

440 court locations with 1,479 judges;
401 commissioners and referees

Line of Appeal   Line of Discretionary review

FIGURE 11.1   **California Court System**

Note: *Death penalty cases are automatically appealed from the superior court directly to the Supreme Court.
Source: California State Constitution.

Three judges consider each case primarily by reading transcripts from the original trial. The appeals courts continue to see a heavy workload in the areas of juvenile cases, civil cases, and criminal cases, with nearly 24,000 cases filed for appeal in 2010.[4]

CALIFORNIA SUPREME COURT: THE LAST RESORT (ALMOST)

Most of the Supreme Court of California's work involves handling appeals passed up from the appellate courts. The only cases that come to this court directly are requests from death-row prisoners asking the court to review their sentence. It consists of a chief justice, now Tani Cantil-Sakauye, the first Asian-Filipina American to serve as chief justice, and six associate justices. If an individual involved in a case at this level is still not satisfied, he or she may choose to appeal to the U.S. Supreme Court. However, cases that raise constitutional questions appropriate to the U.S. Supreme Court are rare, and the state Supreme Court is the final court of appeal for most cases it determines. In 2010, about 9,300 cases were filed for the California Supreme Court's consideration.[5]

THE SELECTION OF JUDGES: A MIX OF APPOINTMENTS AND ELECTIONS

Every California judge must have passed the Bar exam to become an attorney and paid dues to the California Bar Association for at least ten years, and most attorneys who want to serve as judges also have some form of political connection that puts them on the governor's "short list" for appointment. Although trial court judges are theoretically chosen by the voters in nonpartisan elections for six-year terms, in reality, few judges begin their careers by running for office. When Superior Court judgeships are vacant as a result of death, retirement, or an expansion of the court system, these vacancies are filled by the governor, and these appointments do not require confirmation by legislators. Once appointed, the new judge serves until the next election, which is often canceled because no one files to run against the incumbent. Since there are no term limits for judges, those willing to work for public salaries (generally much lower than salaries of private attorneys) can easily sustain a superior court judicial career in California for decades without their names ever appearing on a ballot.

In contrast, for the higher courts, all judges' names eventually appear on the ballot. Appeals court judges and Supreme Court justices are chosen by a method that enhances *gubernatorial* power to influence the judiciary. The three-step process is as follows.

1. Appointment by the governor based on guidance from his or her judicial appointments secretary.

2. Approval by a majority of the Commission on Judicial Appointments, which consists of the chief justice of the state Supreme Court, the senior presiding justice of the district Court of Appeals, and the state's elected attorney general.

3. Election (confirmation) for a 12-year term, with no opposing candidate permitted to run and voters limited to a choice between yes and no. There are no term limits for any California judges.

In making judicial appointments at all levels, governors usually give special consideration to attorneys who have a good rating from the state Bar Association as well as the appropriate political connections. Like the president, the governor can use judicial appointments to promote his or her agenda. The governor's political views can have an enormous impact on the types of judges appointed. Judicial appointments generally tend to represent the more privileged groups in society (who have the financial resources to become attorneys and the connections to be nominated by the governor) and do not fully reflect the ethnic diversity of California's attorneys. Some governors emphasize the importance of diversity when they appoint judges, while others insist that their selections must be "color-blind." In the most recent court data (2011), approximately 74 percent of California judges were white, and approximately 70 percent were male.[6]

Once appointed and confirmed, few justices have trouble winning confirmation from the voters. With the unusual exception of the "Dump Rose Bird" campaign (1986), neither voters nor election strategists have spent much time worrying about who sits on the California courts. State Supreme Court Chief Justice Rose Bird, appointed by Democratic Governor Jerry Brown during his 1974–1982 governorship, became the symbol of "soft" liberalism regarding capital punishment and was unseated by voters after 11 years. The successful campaign to unseat her also resulted in the voters' removal of two other justices appointed by Democratic governors, allegedly for also being too soft on crime. When these three liberal justices lost their posts, Republican governor George Deukmejian replaced them with three conservative justices. Governor Jerry Brown's first appointment in his current term was Goodwin Liu, a former UC Berkeley law professor who has received the highest possible rating by the American Bar Association.

With rare exceptions at the local court level, voters generally support gubernatorial appointments and keep most incumbent judges in office. Voter interest in judicial contests is low, and voters often feel that they are casting a ballot blindly when they vote on judges. Few Californians pay attention to the quality of their judges until they need to appear in court and see a judge in action. Like all other elected officials in California, all judges, including state Supreme Court justices, are subject to voter recall, but this process has rarely occurred.

COMPARED TO CALIFORNIA

**JUDICIAL SELECTION PATTERNS IN THE FEDERAL
SYSTEM AND SELECTED STATES**

United States: President nominates, U.S. Senate confirms by majority vote

California: Governor appoints, followed by nonpartisan election process

Alabama: *Partisan elections*

Connecticut: Election by legislature

Source: Dennis L. Desang and James J. Gosling, *Politics and Policy in American States and Communities* (New York: Pearson/Longman, 2008), p. 388.

Think Critically: How much should the general public influence the selection and retention of judges? Should judges be protected from elections?

THE NONELECTORAL REMOVAL OF JUDGES: RARE BUT POSSIBLE

Another method to remove judges is the Commission on Judicial Performance, which can force a judge out even when elected by the voters. The commission includes both judges and nonlawyers appointed by the governor and legislature. Its primary task is to investigate complaints about judicial misconduct and, if circumstances indicate, to recommend that the state Supreme Court remove a judge from office.

The commission receives hundreds of complaints each year about judges. Misconduct charges that may be brought against judges include accusations of racial or gender bias, substance abuse, verbal abuse, accepting bribes, personal favoritism, and even senility. The process of being investigated often results in the voluntary resignation or retirement of the judge in question, thus saving the judge the embarrassment of being forced out of office.

THE JUDICIAL COUNCIL: RUNNING A COMPLEX SYSTEM

The 21 voting members of the Judicial Council are empowered to evaluate and improve the administration of justice in the state. Made up of judges, attorneys, and legislative appointees, the council analyzes the workloads of the courts, recommends reorganizations to improve efficiency, and establishes many of the rules of court procedure. In July 2011, in response to a 10 percent cut in court funding by the legislature and governor, the Judicial Council had the painful task of reducing services in the California courts, leading to layoffs and wage cuts for employees and further delays for the public when seeking help through the courts.[7]

SELECTING OUR JUDGES

Viewpoint: The voters should not be involved in judicial elections; they don't know enough about the judges on the ballot.

- Judges should be selected for their qualifications.
- The governor and his judicial appointments staff are the best people to select judges.
- Judges should not be subject to the expensive and confusing election process.

Viewpoint: The vote of the people ensures judicial responsiveness to the public.

- California is proud that the voters have a role in all branches of government.
- The voters should always be able to remove judges if they are not serving the public.
- Judges will perform better knowing that they are subject to voter approval.

Ask Yourself: Do I know enough when my ballot choices include judges? How do I decide my vote?

JUDICIAL POWER: WHO HAS IT AND HOW THEY USE IT

While judges at the local level do not permanently affect questions of constitutionality or set policy through their decisions, the appellate justices and state Supreme Court justices can create legal precedents for California through their written decisions. Because these justices wield such power, governors should choose them carefully. However, governors have their own political preferences. They realize that a judgeship will probably last much longer than their term as governor, and they select justices whose overall political views are compatible with their own, expecting these justices to make legal decisions that meet their political goals. Of course, over time, some appointees disappoint the governors who put them there by making decisions contrary to the wishes of their "patrons."

Six of the seven current members of the state Supreme Court were appointed by Republican governors. Four of the seven are women, one of whom is a lesbian, and four of the justices are Asian Americans. On most issues, their judicial views are similar, with most of them being moderate and pragmatic rather than driven by sharp ideological concerns.

Although individuals who have been in California courtrooms and seen judicial authority in action may feel intimidated or powerless, the public must remember that its electoral choice for governor determines the tone of the judicial branch. If one wants liberal judges, one must elect liberal governors, and the same is true for conservatives. If one wants more women and ethnic minorities represented on the bench, one must evaluate the records and promises of gubernatorial candidates regarding judicial appointments. Similarly, if one believes that justice is color-blind, one must try to elect a candidate who promises to select judges without regard to gender or ethnicity. The important element is the citizen's awareness of the connection between voting for governor and the quality of justice in California.

QUESTIONS TO CONSIDER

Using Your Text and Your Own Experiences

1. Compare and contrast the federal judicial system with California's judicial system in terms of how judges are selected, their length of service, and so on.

2. What is the role of the governor in the judicial branch? Does the governor have too much power? How do voters get involved in judicial selection?

3. Debate the pros and cons of California's judicial confirmation elections. Is judicial independence compromised by this system?

ENJOYING MEDIA

Movies to See and Web sites to Explore

California Court system   courtinfo.ca.gov
This Web site gives good information about how Californians can do business in our judicial system as well as the latest statistics from the judicial branch.

California Law References   leginfo.ca.gov/calaw.html
This Web site includes access to all the laws of the state. California Law consists of 29 codes, covering various subject areas and including thousands of statutes we must obey.

The Rodney King Case: What the Jury Saw in California v. Powell, Dominic Palumbo, 1992
A bystander with a video camera caught the images of four white policemen beating Rodney King, a black motorist, and the jury's acquittal of the four officers on charges of brutality resulted in the 1992 uprisings in Los Angeles. This Court TV film includes expert analysis to make the jury's legal process understandable to the viewer.

ENDNOTES

1. "Foundations for a New Century," *Judicial Council of California*, Administrative Office of the Courts, 2000 Court Statistics Report, 2002. http://www.courtinfo.ca.gov.

2. About California Courts, updated September 2010. http://www.courts.ca.gov/2113.htm.

3. Nick Wilson, "SLO Judges' Voluntary Pay Cut Saves California $40,000," *San Luis Obispo Tribune*, February 16, 2011. http://www.sanluisobispo.com/2011/02/15/1485061/san-luis-obispo-judges-voluntary.html.

4. "Fact Sheet, Introduction," California Judicial Branch, September 2010. http://www.courts.ca.gov/documents/csr2010intro.pdf.

5. Ibid.

6. Demographic Data on Race, Ethnicity and Gender of California Judges, December 31, 2009, p. 1. http://www.courts.ca.gov/documents/2010DemographicReport.pdf.

7. Maura Dolan and Victoria Kim, "Budget Cuts to Worsen Court Delays," *Los Angeles Times*, July 20, 2011, p. A1.

CHAPTER TWELVE

Criminal Justice and Civil Law

We've created 10,000 new jobs in the prison system and financed those jobs by cutting 10,000 positions out of the university and state college system.
  —Bill Lockyer, California Treasurer

All the vast machinery of the judicial system and its related components, including the judges, attorneys, bailiffs, stenographers, police, jails, wardens, and parole officers (to name a few), serve to facilitate two basic types of legal procedures: civil litigation and criminal prosecutions. For many Californians, their maximum contact with the entire judicial/ legal system is their occasional jury duty. For others, their lives are profoundly affected by the structures and processes of the criminal justice system and the civil courts.

CRIMINAL JUSTICE: AN OXYMORON?

Depending on the severity of the act, crimes are normally defined as felonies, misdemeanors, or infractions. *Infractions* are most often violations of traffic laws, whereas *misdemeanors* encompass "less serious" crimes such as shoplifting and public drunkenness. *Felonies*, the most serious crimes and potentially punishable by a year or more in state prison, include both violent and nonviolent crimes.

Like people everywhere, Californians are concerned about protecting themselves from crime. Elaborate alarm systems, gated communities for the wealthy, and a general fear factor permeate daily life. Ballot initiatives such as the "three-strikes" law (1994) created lifetime sentences for a criminal with three felony convictions, but implementation has proven problematic and numerous amendments to that law have been discussed. Except for China and the entire United States, California has the largest penal system in the world. Over 171,000 inmates are housed in 33 prisons, and another 125,000 parolees fall under the jurisdiction of the Department of Corrections and Rehabilitation.[1] Many of the prisoners are nonviolent felons whose life sentences cost taxpayers $500,000–$1 million per inmate.[2]

Despite a multimillion-dollar prison construction program, usually in rural locations where prison jobs support the local economy, California's prisons remain tremendously overcrowded, with periodic outbreaks of violence—in some cases involving accusations that prison guards instigated the trouble. Due to serious concerns about health conditions in the state prisons, federal judges have ordered that prison population be reduced.[3] Various schemes have emerged about how to reduce the number of prisoners, including early release of less violent felons, use of county jails to house felons, or even sending felons to out-of-state prisons. However, it is not clear how exactly the cash-strapped state can manage its huge prison system, and opinion polls indicate that Californians do not want to pay more taxes for prisons, preferring instead to revise sentencing for nonviolent criminals.[4]

Victims of violent crime are entitled to restitution paid by inmates out of their prison wages and family financial gifts, but many crime victims never receive the funds designated for burials, grief counseling, and lost wages. Table 12.1 lists statistics about the California Department of Corrections and Rehabilitation.

CRIME AND ITS VICTIMS: TECHNOLOGY ADVANCES, FEARS REMAIN

California crime rates tend to decline during economic good times, but even when employment opportunities are plentiful, not everyone is able or willing to earn an honest living. Those who adopt long-term criminal lifestyles, including drug dealers, gang leaders, and others, may show no interest in turning over a new leaf and leaving a life of crime. Lack of education plays a key role; the average reading level of criminals in California's prisons is seventh grade (see Table 12.1). Most experts believe that educational and job opportunities can keep young people on a legal path, but political decisions often undermine the funds for such programs. Public fears of violent crime have led to a series of ballot initiatives, including Proposition 21 (2000), which requires juveniles aged 14 or older to be tried as adults for murder, and which increases penalties for gang-related offenses.

Californians worried about violent crime do not necessarily agree on solutions. While opinion polls repeatedly indicate that a large majority support gun control, the vocal minority of gun rights supporters continues to lobby against any restrictions. Communities plagued by crime have tried everything from forming Neighborhood Watch committees, which try to link neighbors in a network of alert watchfulness, to demanding speed bumps and private gates. Some local governments, including Oakland, Pasadena, and many others, have responded by initiating "community policing," a

TABLE 12.1	

California Department of Corrections and Rehabilitation, 2009

Budget	*$10.6 billion*
Portion of state general fund	6.2% (2002–2003)
Average yearly cost	$49,000 per inmate
Staff	63,050 in institutions, parole supervision, and administration
Facilities	33 state prisons
	40 wilderness area camps
	12 community correctional facilities
	5 prisoner mother facilities
Inmate population	159,390 in all institutions
	94% male, 6% female
	39% Latino, 30% black,
	26% white, 6% other
Offense	53% violent crime
	21% property crime
	18% drugs
	7% other
Average reading level	Seventh grade
Special security lifers	27,358
Condemned to death penalty	678
On parole	123,597

Source: California Department of Corrections and Rehabilitation, 2009, http://www.cdcr.ca.gov

system designed to improve communication between neighborhoods and their police force.[5]

Unfortunately, the responsiveness of government agencies sometimes depends on a community's political clout. In low-income areas with little political influence, residents often feel neglected by public safety agencies and do not have the money to purchase alternative sources of protection. More affluent communities have the funds to build gates and walls as well as to hire private security companies to patrol their streets. Underfunding is often blamed for the lack of adequate public policing, even while many cities spend millions defending their undertrained law enforcement officers from a variety of lawsuits, including accusations of racial and gender discrimination and various forms of police abuse.

Because most people worry more about violent crime, Californians have just begun to realize the impacts of some new kinds of white-collar crimes. Recent technologies have fueled a stunning rise in identity theft and credit card fraud, while more traditional larcenies continue to cheat ignorant victims through pyramid investment schemes, phony mortgage loans, fraudulent land sales, staged auto accidents, and other illegal and unethical ways to part people from their money. Although most white-collar crime is nonviolent, sometimes auto insurance scam artists cause innocent people to die when they create accidents in order to file personal injury lawsuits. Victims of white-collar crime are often the elderly, immigrants, or the uneducated. Those who use credit cards frequently, especially in gas stations, are also advised to use extra caution against fraud.

The media feed public fears by emphasizing crime as "news," often ignoring more important political news. Since much of violent crime is linked to drug abuse, illegal drug dealing, and domestic violence, the courts are experimenting with "collaborative courts" that involve treatment providers and close monitoring of offenders.[6] Some politicians continue to remind the public that it costs taxpayers about $49,000 per year to keep the average convict in prison, while the state currently spends about $8,594 on a public school child and $4,500 on a community college student. As a result of the three-strikes initiative (1994), state prisons are full of over 27,000 aging "lifers" whose medical and other specialized care costs nearly $80,000 per convict per year.[7]

THE CRIMINAL JUSTICE PROCESS: A SYSTEM TO AVOID

In many cases, crimes occur and are not reported, or they are reported but no suspect is arrested. In the cases where an arrest is made, the arresting officer often has the option of "naming" the crime by labeling it either a misdemeanor or a felony. If a person is arrested for a felony, the county district attorney's office must decide whether to file the felony charge. In cases without witnesses willing to testify, filing charges becomes a questionable proposition in which tax dollars may be spent on a trial only to arrive at an inconclusive outcome. Because of the strength of some gangs, witnesses are often afraid to testify against someone who could take revenge on the witness or a witness' family member.

Under federal constitutional rights, persons accused of crimes are entitled to speedy trials and a public defender. Judges under budget constraints are often eager to reduce the court workload through a variety of tools. One method of reducing trials is the *plea bargain*, in which the accused person's defense attorney can cut a deal with prosecutors and receive a reduced sentence in exchange for eliminating a full

FIGURE 12.1 **California's Correctional Facilities**

Source: California Department of Corrections.

trial. Defendants with adequate funds may be represented by a private attorney; most accused persons, however, must rely on overworked public defenders to handle their cases. Trials may be decided by either a judge or a jury, depending on the preference of the defendant and his or her attorney. If a jury is used, the entire jury must agree on the final verdict while the judge determines the sentence. The sole exception to this rule is in capital (death penalty) cases, in which the jury, again by unanimous vote, has the duty to recommend either the death penalty or life in prison. (Figure 12.1 shows the locations of prisons in the California system.)

CIVIL LAW: SOLVING PROBLEMS THROUGH THE COURTS

Whereas criminal law deals with matters that are considered injurious to the people of the state of California, civil matters involve any disputes between parties which cannot be resolved without legal assistance. Parties involved in such disputes can include individuals, business entities, and government agencies. The range of civil legal matters includes such cases as dissolution of marriage, child custody, personal injury (including automobile accidents), malpractice, workers' compensation, breach of contract, bankruptcy, and many more. In these cases, the court's role frequently is to determine liability and to assess damages, often amounting to millions of dollars. In contrast to criminal defendants, the defendant (person being sued) in a civil case has no right to government-funded legal defense.

Most civil lawsuits never reach a court but rather are settled outside the courtroom by the attorneys. Those that do go to trial may be decided by a judge or a jury, with only a two-thirds majority of jurors required to agree in order to decide the outcome. Because civil cases have no constitutional protection against delay, waiting for a court date can sometimes last years. One way to avoid the delay is an out-of-court *settlement* arranged by the attorneys of the parties involved. These settlements often save time, money, and aggravation for both the *plaintiff* and the *defendant*. Another alternative to the long wait is to pay private judges to settle disputes outside the public judicial system. Private judges can also prevent public or media access to details about the lives of wealthy or well-known individuals. This *privatization* of the civil legal system may result in speedier justice for those able to buy a judge's time while those involved in the public system continue to wait years for their case to come to court.

JURIES: THE CITIZEN'S DUTY

California has two types of juries: the most common, the trial jury, and the less well-known grand jury. In both cases, jurors must be U.S. citizens. The county grand jury, made up of a select group of citizens nominated by superior court judges, serves a one-year term for minimal compensation, thus leaving this task to the affluent or retired. Their purpose is to investigate possible criminal activity and bring *indictments* against either public officials or private parties.

Unlike the grand jury which is selected for a year, trial juries are created for the length of a particular trial. For felony trials, the jury consists of 12 citizens, while as few as nine jurors may try a misdemeanor case or a civil trial. Trial juries are found through both voter registration and motor vehicle license lists. County courts send out notices asking citizens to serve; penalties for failure to respond have increased to $1,500 in some counties.

The jury system has been criticized for many reasons, including the low compensation ($15 per day), the potential for emotional (rather than rational) decision making, and the poor use of jurors' time when they do agree to serve. Recent efforts to improve the situation include the one-day-or-one-trial system (which allows people to get back to work more quickly), the use of pager and call-in systems to avoid long waits, and improved jury waiting areas. Although jury duty is often perceived as a boring chore, the jury system is still considered one of the genuine advantages of living in a democratic society with a constitutional right to an impartial jury and due process of law.[8]

DEBATING THE ISSUES

JURY DUTY

Viewpoint: Every citizen, no matter what his or her level of education, should do their share and serve on a jury once per year.

- The American tradition expects every citizen to do jury duty.
- No one, no matter how rich or poor, educated or ignorant, should avoid jury duty.

Viewpoint: Jury duty should only be required from citizens with a certain level of education (i.e., high school diploma).

- Uneducated jurors make poor decisions, so all jurors should have a high school diploma.
- Juries decide complex issues and undereducated people cannot do the job correctly.

Ask Yourself: Am I prepared to serve on a jury? If not, what should I do to be better prepared?

QUESTIONS TO CONSIDER

Using Your Text and Your Own Experiences

1. What are some of the root causes of our overloaded criminal justice system? What can be done about solving them?
2. What are some alternatives to our overloaded civil courts? How else can problems be resolved between individuals or organizations?
3. What can be done to increase the number of people who serve on juries? Share your experiences, if any, doing jury duty.

ENJOYING MEDIA

Movies to See and Web sites to Explore

Central California Free Legal Aid (civil cases)   centralcallegal.org
A nonprofit law firm providing free legal assistance to low-income people in California's Central Valley.

California Department of Corrections   cdcr.ca.gov
and Rehabilitation
All the data on the state's correction system, including juvenile justice, job opportunities, and legal issues impacting the prisons and related systems.

State Bar   calbar.ca.gov
The State Bar is the organization for attorneys in California; the Web site includes information and attorney referral services.

Training Day, Antoine Fugua, 2001
An unsettling depiction of the drug scene of South Central Los Angeles and the role of the Los Angeles Police Department as seen through the eyes of a new officer. Raises issues of police integrity in one of the highest crime areas of California.

Real Time, Lee Miller, 2002
This documentary explores the reality of adolescent life in prison at the California Youth Authority (CYA) Stockton facility. Kids between ages 11 and 18 with violent felony convictions struggle to understand their past behavior while the CYA staff try to prepare them for life outside prison.

The Legacy: Murder & Media, Politics & Prison, Michael J. Moore, 1999
This PBS documentary exposes the disturbing story behind the passage of California's stringent three-strikes law. Judges, legal analysts, and state officials describe how criminal justice policy is debated in today's media-saturated political climate—particularly in a state where more money is spent on building prisons than on education.

ENDNOTES

1. California Department of Corrections and Rehabilitation, Fourth Quarter 2008 Facts and Figures, http://www.cdcr.ca.gov/Divisions_Boards/Adult_Operations/docs/Fourth_Quarter_2008_Facts_and_Figures.pdf.
2. Greg Krikorian, "Three Strikes Law Has No Effect, Study Finds," *Los Angeles Times*, March 2, 1999, p. A3.
3. Huffington Post, Adam Weintraub, California Prison Overcrowding: Brown unveils Plan to Slash Prison Population, June 8, 2011. http://www.huffingtonpost.com/2011/06/07/california-prison-overcrowding_n_872785.html.
4. Jack Dolan, "No New Taxes for Prisons, Residents Say," *Los Angeles Times*, July 21, 2011, p. A1.
5. City of Pacific Grove, Community Policing, 2005. http://www.ci.pg.ca.us/police/compolicing.htm,
6. *Collaborative Justice Courts*, California Courts, 2011. http://www.courts.ca.gov/programs-collabjustice.htm.
7. California Department of Corrections and Rehabilitation, Fourth Quarter 2008 Facts and Figures, http://www.cdcr.ca.gov/Adult_Operations/docs/Fourth_Quarter_2009_Facts_and_Figures.pdf.
8. Amendments V and VI, U.S. Constitution.

CHAPTER THIRTEEN

City Governments: Providing the Basics

> The power of local governments to make choices about the level and quality of local services has eroded over the last 20 years. Local communities should be given more local control.
>
> —Constitutional Revision Commission, 1996

There are several types of local government in California—county, city, and special districts—as well as regional agencies that attempt to coordinate their policies. Of these, city government is probably the local government agency that is most accessible to the public. Cities have enormous responsibilities to their residents but are severely constrained by budget limitations, especially the loss of local property tax revenues caused by Proposition 13. As in other levels of government, finding the best ways to generate revenues and provide needed services is an ongoing battle among city officials.

HOW CITIES ARE CREATED: IT'S NOT EASY

With the exceptions of some of the older cities, such as Los Angeles, San Francisco, and San Jose, which received their charters from the state when California was admitted to the Union, most cities in California "incorporate" when the residents decide they need their own local government. Before incorporation, areas that are not cities are called *unincorporated areas*, and their residents normally receive basic urban services from the county in which they live. Occasionally, an unincorporated area is simply annexed, or joined with, a nearby city by a majority vote of that territory's residents along with the approval of the adjacent city.

Perhaps the most common reason residents initiate the incorporation process is that the county government, which provides their services, is too far away and unresponsive. If residents believe that police and fire protection is inadequate, or that planning and zoning issues are not well handled, or even that rents are too high in the area, they may organize to create their own city in which they can elect their own officials to control these issues. Of course, residents who want their own city government must realize that there are costs involved in running a city, and they must be prepared to tax themselves to pay for city services. They must also agree to share their tax revenues with the county so that it can maintain its countywide services to their residents.[1]

Incorporation begins with a petition signed by at least 25 percent of the registered voters in an area. The petition is then submitted to the Local Agency Formation Commission (LAFCO). Each county has a LAFCO to analyze all issues relating to incorporation, boundary changes, and annexations. The LAFCO must determine the economic feasibility of a proposed city. If the LAFCO decides that cityhood would be financially viable, it authorizes an election in which cityhood can be approved by a simple majority. Once a city exists, even if it is very poorly managed, it is virtually impossible for it to be "disincorporated." A legislative effort to dissolve the city of Vernon due to fiscal corruption was defeated after much lobbying by various interest groups.[2]

DEBATING THE ISSUES

GROWTH OF CITIES

Viewpoint: Cities should regulate urban growth through careful land-use decisions about size of homes, number of housing units per acre, etc.

- Cities must control their land use in order to encourage mass transit, reduced air pollution, and minimize the impacts of natural disasters.
- Cities must control their land use in order to provide affordable housing.
- Cities must control their land use in order to create the right balance of business and housing opportunities.

Viewpoint: Cities should let the private market determine what gets built.

- Government regulation of land use has resulted in inadequate housing supplies.
- Government regulation of land use has harmed businesses that cannot prosper due to overregulation.
- Government regulation of land use is a contradiction to the free enterprise system and philosophy.

Ask Yourself: What choices can I make about my education, career, and housing in order to have a better quality of life?

CITY RESPONSIBILITIES: MANY TASKS, LIMITED REVENUES

Whether a city is a "general law" city that derives all its powers from statutes passed by the state legislature, or a "charter" city that has its own locally written constitution, all cities share similar tasks and responsibilities. Basic, day-to-day necessities such as sewage and garbage disposal, police and fire protection, libraries, streets and traffic control, recreation and parks facilities, and planning and zoning policy form the backbone of city services. In many cities, some of these services are provided through contracts with the county to purchase services such as law enforcement, fire protection, and street maintenance.

Until 1978, cities obtained about one-fourth of their revenues from local property taxes. After Proposition 13 slashed this source, cities cut back many services and turned to the state capitol in Sacramento for assistance. However, Sacramento does not provide resources comparable to those lost from local property taxes. To fill in the budget gaps, most cities now rely on utility and sales taxes, as well as an array of increased fees, including those for building permits, recreational facilities, real estate transfers, garbage collection, and more. Business licenses, parking meters, traffic fines, and limited federal grants are additional sources of revenue.

Because sales taxes are often the easiest to collect, city zoning decisions now contribute to "the fiscalization of land use," which promotes commercial developments at the expense of housing. Neighboring cities fight each other to see which city can offer more financial incentives to the developer of an auto dealer, movie complex, sports arena, or shopping mall, because these land uses will provide sales tax revenue. Rarely do cities offer support for developers of affordable housing, one of the state's most urgent needs.

During a slowdown in the economy, cities, like all government entities, find their tax revenues inadequate for public needs. Police departments usually obtain the largest chunk of city monies, leaving fire services, libraries, parks and recreation, and other departments to battle for their share of the pie.

FORMS OF CITY GOVERNMENT: TWO BASICS WITH VARIATIONS

Although there are numerous local versions, city government in California falls within two broad types. The *mayor–council* variety entails a separation of powers between the mayor, who has executive responsibility for the functioning of most city departments, and the council, which enacts legislation known as *ordinances*. If the mayor has the power to veto ordinances and to appoint department heads, the government is known as a strong mayor–council variety; if not, it is a weak mayor–council system. Larger cities sometimes include aspects of both the strong and weak systems.

The *council–manager* type of government gives the city council both executive and legislative power, but the council exercises its executive power by appointing a professionally trained city manager to coordinate and administer city departments. These city managers are usually very well paid (many earn more than the state's governor) and serve as long as the council wishes. In this form of government, there is a ceremonial mayor with no executive powers who is merely one of the council members. This mayoral position is typically rotated around the council, with each member serving a year and then returning to his or her regular council status. The mayor continues to hold a vote equal to that of every other member of the city council.

Los Angeles and San Francisco employ the mayor–council form, while Oakland, San Jose, and Torrance are among the 90 percent of all cities in the state that use the council–manager form.[3] Under both systems, most cities have a city clerk, attorney, treasurer or controller, and planning commission, with all but the last-named elected directly by voters. The most common departments are police, fire, public works, recreation and parks, and building and zoning. These are usually headed by high-level civil servants or appointees and monitored by advisory commissions appointed by the mayor and/or the council.

In terms of the quality of daily life, a resident with a complaint about city services should do some research regarding the structure of city government in order to get the fastest and most helpful response. If the bureaucracy that controls the street cleaning services is not responsive, the resident with a dirty street must understand which of the elected officials is most directly responsible for that section of the city in order to obtain better street cleaning. City employees, though generally hardworking and concerned, may go the extra mile if a city council member makes a special request for a constituent. Of course, providing service to individuals can sometimes lead to unethical favors for constituents. If individuals ask for special consideration, such as permission to build larger buildings than current codes permit, outraged citizens may demand investigations of elected officials who try to gain political support through this abuse of power.[4]

CITY POLITICS: POWER BLOCS IN COMPETITION

The forces that influence city politics are even more varied than the forms of city government. Homeowners, builders, city employee unions, historic preservationists, environmentalists, realtors, street vendors, renters, and landlords are among the groups that vie for clout in the city's decision-making process. In city elections, as in most political campaigns, incumbents tend to have the advantage, but an incumbent who has made enough enemies can be ousted by a well-organized challenger. In some cities, term limits have been enacted and opportunities

COMPARED TO CALIFORNIA

METROPOLITAN AREA POPULATIONS, 2008

Tokyo: 35 million

Mexico City: 19 million

New York City: 8 million

Los Angeles: 4 million

San Francisco: 800,000

Bakersfield: 247,000

Source: Lester R. Brown, *Plan B 2.0: Rescuing a Planet under Stress and a Civilization in Trouble* (New York: W.W. Norton & Co., 2006), http://factfinder.census.gov

Think Critically: How is daily life impacted by the population density of a city? What size city do you live in? What is your ideal size for a city?

for newcomers have increased. Ironically, despite the many issues determined by city councils, some cities have canceled elections due to incumbents running with no opposition.[5]

One factor in city politics is whether council members are elected *at-large* or *district-based*. In most of California's nearly 500 cities, council members are elected at-large; that is, they may live anywhere in the city. Only a few cities use district-based elections, which divide the city into geographic areas from which council members are elected. (Figure 13.1 shows the 15 city council districts of Los Angeles.) For years, the argument for at-large elections was that the most qualified people could get into office regardless of their address. However, this often results in large sections of cities, particularly those inhabited by ethnic minorities, not being represented on the council owing to the financial advantages of whites from other areas who run for office. The California Voting Rights Act of 2001 requires that local governments prove that their at-large elections do not create "racial polarization," and lawsuits have been filed to force the city of Modesto, the Hanford Unified School District, and other Central Valley local jurisdictions to create district elections.[6] In general, most cities that change from at-large to district-based elections usually experience an increase in ethnic diversity on their councils.

Another factor in how well a council represents city residents is whether the council job is full time or part time. In most cities, serving on the city council is a form of community volunteerism, with a small stipend paid for countless hours of city-related tasks. In these cases, those able to run and serve as council members tend to be affluent businesspeople or retired persons. In rare cases, "part-time" elected officials have paid themselves huge illegal salaries. Residents of the city

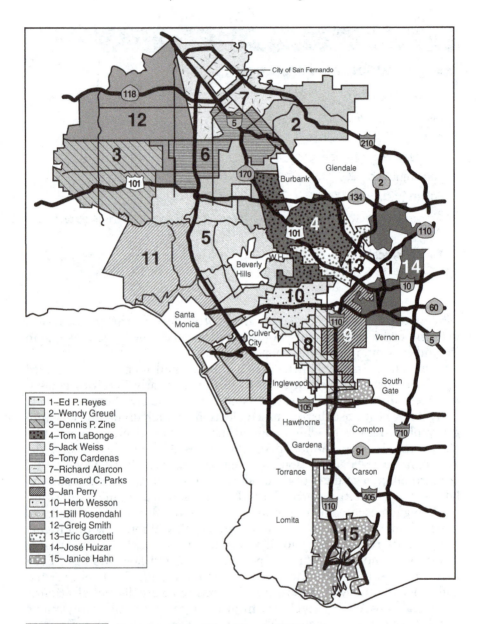

FIGURE 13.1 **Los Angeles City Council Districts**

Source: City Clerk, Los Angeles.

of Bell rose up in rage when they realized what their city officials were earning, and those officials were removed from office, with some being arrested on charges of misappropriation of public funds.[7]

Despite occasional bursts of civic involvement such as occurred in Bell when the salary scandal became public, most council business is often handled without much public debate or attention. While few people take advantage of the opportunity, California's "open meeting law" (also known as the Brown Act) enables any member of the public to speak to an elected body. The only issues that elected bodies may hear in private (closed) session involve personnel matters, legal actions, labor negotiations, or property deals. All other matters must be discussed in the view of the public. Public notice of meetings and their agendas must be made available in advance, although these notices are often tucked away in little-read newspapers. In some cities, cable television offers residents a chance to see their city council in action.

As in all levels of government, city policies are often determined by those who are most able to contribute to campaigns. It is at the city level, however, that well-organized nonaffluent groups can also get involved most successfully. Environmentalists in San Francisco helped promote the city's successful composting program in which "green waste" is collected and turned into fertilizer,[8] while Fresno's farmers and residents gained the city's support for a federal lawsuit challenging water allocations for the San Joaquin Valley.[9]

Cities are often the arena for battles over land use and open space, with developers defending their proposed construction projects against opposition from environmentalists and homeowners, as well as public agencies that believe that more buildings will bring increased demands on public services, greater traffic, and deterioration of the natural environment. At the same time, development creates jobs, and many cities are opening their doors for construction projects despite some community opposition.[10]

Although many Californians take their city services for granted, the quality of city functions is actually determined by the quality of the elected officials and civil servants of any particular city. Disparities in the quality of these services are part of the reason for the vast differentials in property values around the state. A desirable home is a home in a well-run city, and a well-run city is usually one with large numbers of active community members who demand that public officials be accountable to the people.

QUESTIONS TO CONSIDER

Using Your Text and Your Own Experiences

1. What are the responsibilities of city government? What tax resources can city officials use to accomplish their goals?

2. Compare and contrast the two forms of city government. Which does your city use? What are the pros and cons of each?

3. Discuss the pros and cons of at-large vs. district-based city elections. Which does your city use? Which do you think is best?

ENJOYING MEDIA

Movies to See and Web sites to Explore

League of California Cities   cacities.org
Information about California's 478 cities and how they work together to advocate in Sacramento and Washington for their concerns.

City Data   city-data.com/city/California.html
Links to every city in California, with population, weather, real estate, and other useful information.

Chinatown, Roman Polanski, 1974
The Oscar-winning classic blends murder mystery with municipal corruption involved in bringing water to the desert of Los Angeles in the early 1900s. Some of the political events are based on the true story of how William Mulholland, Los Angeles' chief engineer, developed the L.A. Aquaduct, bringing water from Mono Lake by draining the lake and destroying the Owens Valley farming community.

Neighborhoods: The Hidden Cities of San Francisco—The Castro, Peter L. Stein, 1998.
Part of a series from KQED (Northern California Public Broadcasting), which explores San Francisco's cultural, social, and economic history. This segment describes the transformation of the Castro area from an immigrant working community into the world's first gay hometown during the 1980s.

ENDNOTES

1. Frank Messina, "Drives toward Cityhood Slowed by Revenue Law," *Los Angeles Times*, July 15, 1997, p. A13.
2. *KTLA News Online*, Lawmakers Vote to Dissolve Scandal Plagued City of Vernon, April 28, 2011. http://www.ktla.com/news/landing/ktla-vernon-take-over,0,1617938.story.
3. Ed Goldman, "Out of the Sandbox: Sacramento City Politics May Go Bigtime," *California Journal*, May 1993, p. 17.
4. Will Rogers, "Intimidation of City Staff Is Rampant, Pair Says," *Glendale News Press*, July 16, 1997, p. A1.
5. Douglas P. Shuit, "Lack of Interest Cancels Some Local Elections," *Los Angeles Times*, February 21, 1999, p. A1.
6. Rod Pacheco, California City News, *Guest Feature: California's Voting Rights Act and the New Lawsuits*, February 28, 2011. http://californiacitynews.typepad.com/californiacitynewsorg/2011/02/gu.html.
7. Eight Arrested in California City Scandal, *MSNBC*, September 21, 2010. http://www.msnbc.msn.com/id/39291038/ns/us_news-crime_and_courts/t/arrested-calif-city-salary-scandal.

8. Jane Kay, "San Francisco's Scraps Bring Joy to Area Farmers," *San Francisco Chronicle,* April 1, 2009, p. 3.
9. "City of Fresno Joins Lawsuit Challenging Water Supply Allocations," City of Fresno Web site, August 10, 2009. http://www.fresno.gov/News/PressReleases/2009/WaterLawsuit.htm.
10. Arash Markazi, "LA Council Passes AEG's Stadium Plan," *ESPN Los Angeles.Com*, August 10, 2011. http://espn.go.com/los-angeles/nfl/story/_/id/6847826/la-council-passes-framework-deal-nfl-venue.

CHAPTER FOURTEEN

Counties, Special Districts, and Education K–Graduate

Californians' support for maintaining K–12 spending remains strong … Public school parents are noticing the impact of state budget cuts on their children's schools.

—Mark Baldassare, Public Policy Institute of California

Californians rarely realize how many governmental jurisdictions impact their lives. The state has a hodge-podge of over 7,000 local governments, with a total of more than 15,000 local elected officials, who often work to provide services duplicated by an agency a few miles away.[1] While the concept "county" is generally recognized (although its functions are mysterious), the various types of special districts can be truly obscure. On the other hand, most Californians have contact with the various educational systems, ranging from local K–12 (kindergarten through 12 grade) school districts, local community colleges, and the two public university systems, California State University (23 campuses) and the University of California (10 campuses).

COUNTIES: MISUNDERSTOOD BUT VITAL ENTITIES

California's 58 counties are administrative subdivisions of the state which come in all shapes and sizes, and their existence as well as their diverse sizes is rooted in the state's early history, rather than any logical system of dividing the state. Los Angeles County, with close to 10 million residents, has more people than over 40 states. San Bernardino County, with its 20,000 square miles, is the largest in the country. In contrast, mountainous Alpine County, which borders Nevada near Lake Tahoe, has about 1,300 residents, and San Francisco, the only combined city-county in the state, comprises only 49 square miles.

For residents of *unincorporated areas*, counties provide the basic urban services: safety, road repair, zoning, libraries, and parks. Counties also dispense another complete set of services to all residents, both those in cities and those in unincorporated regions. These programs include administration of welfare programs such as Temporary Assistance for Needy Families (TANF); supervision of foster care and adoptions of abused or neglected children; maintenance of property ownership, voter registration, and birth and marriage records; prosecution of felonies; operation of the superior court system; provision of health services (including mental health) to the uninsured; and control of public health problems such as highly contagious diseases and outbreaks of food poisoning.

In order to provide these varied services, counties must receive financial support from the state and federal governments. Nationwide welfare programs such as TANF receive substantial funds from the federal government, while the state provides a large measure of funding for the county's health-care programs and the public protection agencies such as courts, district attorney's offices, and county jails. Like the cities, counties have become heavily dependent on Sacramento since Proposition 13. The state's fiscal crisis puts enormous pressures on counties, and cuts in county health and safety services have impacted virtually every Californian.

In addition to budget constraints, another logistical problem facing California's counties is the overlap of services when cities and counties provide identical services in virtually the same community. County sheriffs' departments continue to serve unincorporated areas just blocks from where those same services are provided by city police departments. Some cities prefer to avoid the costs and liability of running their own police or fire departments and become *contract cities*, which purchase these services from the county.

Another ongoing problem for counties is the issue of adequate representation. With the exception of San Francisco, with its combined city-county status and its 11-member board of supervisors, all counties are governed by five-member boards of supervisors, exercising both legislative and executive powers. In less-populated counties, five individuals may be sufficient; in counties such as Los Angeles, five supervisors serving 10 million residents clearly seems inadequate. In addition to electing their supervisors, county voters also usually elect a sheriff, district attorney, and tax assessor.

SPECIAL DISTRICTS: DOING WHAT ONLY THEY CAN DO

Special districts serve the purpose of providing a specific service that no other jurisdiction provides. Special district services include water supplies, street lighting, mosquito abatement, transportation, air quality control, and much more. With over 5,000 special districts, California may take the prize for providing local control of services, but the fiscal consequences are high.[2] Normally, each district performs only one task and yet may have a well-paid staff with travel budgets and perks. Most special districts are governed by the county board of supervisors or their appointees, while some special district boards are elected by the public. Many special district boards operate almost invisibly, making decisions and spending money away from the awareness of the public or media.

Special districts range in size from small cemetery districts to the Metropolitan Water District of Southern California, which serves six counties and wields enormous political clout, especially during drought periods, when the politics of water distribution become most tense. Other large (regional) special districts include the Los Angeles County Metropolitan Transit Authority (METRO) and the Bay Area Rapid Transit District (BART). The many special districts, both large and small, create both confusion and costs for Californians. In response to complaints about expensive bureaucracies, the Constitutional Revision Commission has suggested a massive overhaul of special districts,[3] but as yet, no such changes have been implemented.

EDUCATION DISTRICTS: K–12 AND COMMUNITY COLLEGES

Of all the services provided by local governments, the biggest and most expensive is public education. This is the responsibility of more than 1,100 education districts, including approximately 630 elementary school districts, 115 high school districts, 72 community college districts, and 285 unified districts providing both elementary and high school programs. These districts each have elected boards, ranging from five to seven members, accountable directly to the voters. While about 90 percent of education districts elect their boards *at-large*, others have gone to *by-district* elections, many due to a court ruling that the *at-large* system violates the federal Voting Rights Act and reduces opportunities for Latinos to get elected.[4] In all cases, public K–14 education's chief revenue source is the state (under Proposition 98 funding guarantees), with some monies still derived from local property taxes, some federal funds for specialized programs, and a tiny portion of their budgets from the state lottery.

California's schools were among the best in the nation until Proposition 13 (1978) drastically cut the primary funding source. Since then, California public schools declined in measures such as pupil–teacher ratio, maintenance of school facilities, and number of computers per student. School budgets depend heavily on whether the state economy and budget are flourishing; during recessions, budgets for schools and community colleges get cut along with social services and county governments. Compounding the overall issue about inadequate state funding are the enormous differences in quality between affluent, suburban school districts (where property tax revenues are higher and parents can donate more cash) and the schools in most inner cities. In some large urban areas, many public schools are being converted to *charter schools*, which are free and public, but do not have to follow some of the complex rules of the California Education Code, thus allowing innovation and improvements. Substantial private money has been donated to expand charter schools, although some measurements indicate that the quality of education in charter schools is no better, and sometimes worse, than regular public schools.[5]

Along with the thousand-plus K–12 school districts, 72 community college districts, with a total of 112 colleges, serve the state's adult population. These two-year colleges enable over 2.9 million Californians to earn credits for university transfer, receive vocational training, or learn English as a Second Language and other basic skills. There are no entrance requirements other than being 18 years of age (or, in some cases, being approved to attend at a younger age). Despite substantial fee increases in recent years, California residents still pay lower community college fees than residents of other states, while students from other nations and states pay "out-of-state," tuition which is still considerably less than that of most private colleges. California's community colleges have been hit hard by state budget cuts, and cuts in the public universities have reduced transfer opportunities. Though heavily dependent on state funding, each community college district's specific budget decisions are made by a locally elected board of trustees, which also has the authority to place bond measures on the ballot for college construction programs.

COMPARED TO CALIFORNIA

K–12 SPENDING PER PUPIL, 2007

California: $8,477

Arizona: $7,928

Vermont: $12,093

New Jersey: $14,203

U.S. average: $9,056

Source: U.S. Census Bureau data, 2009, http://nces.ed.gov/pubs2009/revexpdist07/tables/table_03.asp#f1

Think Critically: What would change for California's school children if our K–12 funding were more like New Jersey? What improvements could be made for the increased dollars?

HIGHER EDUCATION: CSU AND UC—ARE THEY STILL PUBLIC UNIVERSITIES?

Both statewide university systems have been identified as among the nation's finest systems, offering world-class educational opportunities. At the same time, budget cuts and fee increases have created difficulties in retaining top faculty, as well as extreme hardship on students. Large salaries paid to top administrators have brought criticism from the public as well as state officials, while students have protested the skyrocketing fees.[6] The original California Master Plan for Higher Education (developed in 1960), which created an almost free higher education structure, including the community colleges and two university systems, was designed to allow open access to all Californians but has been severely undermined by budget cuts to all three sectors.

The governance structure of both university systems is similar: each has a governing board with most of its members appointed by the Governor. These boards, known as the Trustees of the CSU and the Regents of UC, are the highest authority in managing the huge systems and must operate within the budgets provided by the state legislature. Depending upon which governor appoints them, Trustees and Regents may or may not have any educational background, but rather may be campaign supporters with little knowledge of public higher education.

The recent state budget cuts in both university systems leave Regents and Trustees with no options except to determine how to keep operating with ever-diminished funds. At the UCs, student fees (all fees collected at all campuses) now exceed state support, raising the question of whether the UC system is moving into privatization. Already, much of the money going to the UCs comes from private sources, such as research grants to professors, donations from alumni, and revenues from university hospitals (at the five campuses where UC offers medical school). Another way to raise revenue is to admit more out-of-state students who pay much higher fees than California residents; UC Berkeley's Class of 2015 will have 30 percent non-Californians.[7]

REGIONAL AGENCIES: TWO TYPES, SIMILAR CONCERNS

As the problems facing California become more difficult to solve at the city or county level, regional agencies continue their efforts to improve air and water quality, increase transportation options, and manage other "quality of life" concerns. There are two kinds of regional agencies: multi-issue and single-issue. *Multi-issue regional agencies* do studies of traffic congestion, air quality and other important

---

DEBATING THE ISSUES

EDUCATION DISTRICTS

Viewpoint: California's public school system is so dysfunctional that the public systems should be replaced by vouchers and a marketplace of school options.

- Public schools in many places are overcrowded; privatization would encourage many new and less-crowded schools to be developed.
- Public schools do not provide adequate personal attention to students; private schools do.

Viewpoint: Public schools are one of the places that Californians learn to interact with each other and develop tolerance and respect for diversity, and thus public education should be fully funded and supported by Californians.

- Public schools are needed to bring together all kinds of people in preparation for the diversity in the world of work.
- Private schools usually serve only the more functional students; what would happen to those who need special education or other special support?

Ask Yourself: What did my K–12 experience teach me? Did I get a quality education? If not, how can I compensate as an adult?

---

problems, and then create advisory documents for local governments to consider.

Single-issue regional agencies, are like large special districts, with one specific purpose. Air quality management districts, public transportation districts, and water districts are often regional agencies.

QUESTIONS TO CONSIDER

Using Your Text and Your Own Experiences

1. Describe the responsibilities of counties and their funding base. What are the financial challenges facing California counties?

2. Define *special districts* and give several examples. Does California need to revise its approach to providing services through special districts? Explain your answer.

3. What is the governing structure of CSU and UC? How do these two public systems differ from the many private universities in California?

ENJOYING MEDIA

Movies to See and Web sites to Explore

California Special Districts Association   csda.net
The organization of over 1,000 special districts, primarily to share information and advocate for the SDs.

California Department of Education   cde.ca.gov
The state's oversight agency for public K–12 systems.

Community College Chancellors Office   cccco.edu
The coordinating agency for California's 72 community college districts and the 110 community colleges they operate.

California State Association of Counties   csac.counties.org
Advocacy, information, and networking for California's 58 counties.

Erin Brockovich, Steven Soderbergh, 2000
Based on a true story, this film shows the journey of Erin Brockovich, who sued Pacific Gas and Electric over contaminated drinking water in unincorporated Hinkley in the Mojave Desert and won the largest settlement in a lawsuit of its kind in U.S. history. While the events occurred in California's sparsely populated desert region, the underlying problems exist everywhere.

ENDNOTES

1. California Special District Association, What's So Special about Special Districts?, Fourth Edition, October 2010. http://www.csda.net/full-remositoy-menu/func-startdown/12/.
2. "Government in California: Buckling under the Strain," *The Economist*, February 13, 1993, p. 21.
3. California Constitution Revision Commission, p. 74. *1996 http://www.californiacityfinance.com/CCRCfinalrpt.pdf*
4. Mitchell Landsberg, "Making Sure Minorities' Votes Count," *Los Angeles Times*, January 4, 2009, p. B1.
5. Howard Blume, "Charter Group Gets $15 Million," *Los Angeles Times*, August 23, 2011, p. AA3.
6. "Fee Increase Passes Despite Opposition and Protest," *UC AFT*, December 2010. http://ucaft.org/content/fee-increase-passes-despite-opposition-and-protest-0.
7. Larry Gordon, "A First: UC Fees Exceed State Funding," *Los Angeles Times*, August 22, 2011, p.A1.

CHAPTER FIFTEEN

Challenges for California's Future

> In the end, we do not know for sure whether the California public really wants the California dream anymore. The population is too diverse to have a common vision of what it wants to provide to everyone. Some people want the old dream, some want the gated privatized version, and some would like to secede and get away from it all.
>
> —Bruce Cain, U.C. Berkeley Political Scientist

California moves forward into the twenty-first century with a tremendous gap between the state's allocations for public services and the state's continuing needs for housing, education, transportation, water, and energy—all necessities that are not easily provided if government is frozen in old structures and thinking. While some people continue to enjoy the material success that has often defined the California dream, the economic downturn has many Californians feeling that the dream is a myth. With a *polarized* political system, in which "no new taxes" battles with "serve the people," the issue of how to move all Californians forward remains highly partisan and unresolved. A few glimmers of hope exist: Changes in legislative redistricting and primaries may create a more rational legislature, and murmurs of adjustments in Proposition 13 (i.e., split roll tax) could create some stable revenues. What will probably not occur is a decrease in the public's demands for quality education, safe cities, well-maintained highways, and other governmental services.

INTERCONNECTED CHALLENGES: ECONOMY, ENVIRONMENT, AND ENERGY

In the vast forests, along the coast, and in the deserts, valleys, and cities, California's enormous, beautiful, and productive territory is both a benefit and a challenge. As the world is increasingly impacted by global warming, California's water supplies fluctuate from acceptable to at-risk. Floods and droughts are both seen as serious threats to the San Joaquin Delta region, and depleting water sources are reducing agricultural production and causing enormous unemployment among farm laborers in the San Joaquin Valley as well as the Imperial Valley regions.[1]

Recent surveys indicate that Californians are taking global climate change seriously, and a majority support continuing efforts to reduce greenhouse gas emissions, improve energy efficiency, and build public transportation.[2] Energy supplies now include the increased use of solar power, wind turbines, and other renewable alternatives to oil and coal. Virtually all public agencies in the state now require "green building" standards that utilize new construction methods and reduce the need for nonrenewable energy and water.

Even as the energy and environmental issues are debated, California's economy is challenged by *globalization*, in which more jobs are *outsourced* to other states and countries even while the state grows increasingly dependent on foreign imports. Fortunately, the state is still the nation's largest exporter, including agricultural products and entertainment.[3] Nonetheless, the lowest-income Californians are often just one layoff or medical emergency away from financial disaster, and one of the new concepts in developing their financial security is "asset-building," a program of legislation designed to create college savings, retirement resources, and financial literacy for low-earning Californians.[4]

Along with assisting Californians to become more financially stable, other concerns that must be addressed include the needs for an educated workforce; the difficulties created by the cultural diversity that also enriches California life; the conflicts involved in managing a complex ecosystem; and the serious question as to whether California is governable.

WHAT IS AND WHAT COULD BE

California's economy, despite current struggles at almost every economic level, remains diverse and full of potential. Research indicates that despite some issues regarding the "business climate," it is actually California's moderate temperatures (the actual climate) that encourage much of its economic growth.[5] Although recent budget cuts and furloughs make government employment less secure than in previous eras, the public sector still provides over 2.5 million of California's jobs.[6] Public employment usually involves more than minimum wage, while the private sector offers opportunities ranging from corporate millions to sub-minimum wage work, often on the farms and in the sweatshops still found in many

DEBATING THE ISSUES

ENVIRONMENTAL ISSUES

Viewpoint: Government must regulate air quality, carbon emissions, use of public lands, and other issues that impact the environment.

- Only government can protect people from the greed-based decisions of private industry.
- Only government can coordinate business and require appropriate actions to protect the future resources of California.

Viewpoint: The private market should determine how to control pollution and climate change through consumer demand for clean products.

- Government regulation reduces profitability and drives business out of the state.
- Government regulation can backfire and make problems worse.

Ask Yourself: What is my role as an individual in promoting a cleaner, safer environment?

cities. Individual opportunities depend on many factors, among which is educational attainment. In virtually all of the *service industries*, only the highly educated can move into the upper levels, while those whose education is inadequate usually labor for minimum wage or even less. It is projected that by 2025, 41 percent of jobs will require a college degree but only 35 percent of Californians will have one.[7]

Even though some workers have gained a "living wage" through local political action, and some home health workers, security guards, and janitors have won union representation (often leading to better wages and benefits), the gaps between rich and poor are well documented. This produces a highly bifurcated economy that dramatically impacts the social and political system. Voter turnout is always high among the affluent and low among those who are less educated and have lower income. While the upper class votes, the *underclass* often feels powerless and neglects to exercise this right.

Perhaps the lack of political action among the poor can be attributed to their daily struggle to survive. Being poor is difficult, especially in a place where the contrasts with affluence are highly visible. These vast gaps are somewhat similar to the class structure in nondemocratic and nonindustrial societies (the Third World). Most political leaders rarely talk about the consequences of the continuing income disparity, and some believe that poverty is solely the result of individual choices rather than social policy. (Figure 15.1 indicates family income in California by ethnicity.)

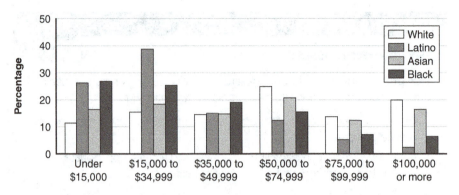

FIGURE 15.1   **Distribution of Family Income in California, 1998**
Source: Public Policy Institute of California.

One contributing factor in this enormous *class gap* is the *regressive* tax system, which taxes the poor a greater share of their income than the rich, in part through subsidizing business and long-time property owners through Proposition 13, and then replacing those tax revenues with utility taxes, sales taxes, public university and college fee increases, and other forms of taxation the poor cannot avoid.

As the industrial economy shifts into a more technologically based system, human adjustments to these changes continue to involve economic and social stress. While new technology brings new opportunities, it also slams the door on many workers. In the growing service sector, technological developments allow fewer people to provide the same services. Entire industries can exist in cyberspace, or in other states or nations, thus providing little employment to Californians. In some cases, these companies exploit California's tax laws in order to avoid paying any

COMPARED TO CALIFORNIA

HIGHER EDUCATION FEES, FALL 2011, PER SEMESTER

University of California: State Resident: $12,192; Out-of-state: $34,164

University of Oregon: State Resident: $8,789; Out-of-state: $27,653

University of Michigan: State Resident: $12,634 Out-of-state: $37,782

Texas A & M University: State Resident: $8,424 Out-of-state: $22,854

Source: College Board, College Search, http://www.collegeboard.com/student/csearch/index.html

Think Critically: How does society benefit from higher education access? Is it important to maintain low fees for public colleges and universities? Why do states charge more to those who come from other states or nations?

taxes to the state. (Amazon.com has been engaged in a fierce political battle over whether it should charge and pay California sales tax.) However, at least some services must be provided where the customer lives: health-care providers, teachers, fast-food servers, and security guards are among the occupations that cannot easily be outsourced.

During good times, when the majority of Californians feel prosperous and secure, there is less obvious prejudice and *scapegoating*. However, during times of economic downturn or insecurity, fears of competition for economic opportunities can cause minor prejudices to become full-fledged ethnic rivalries. As more and more Californians are "new neighbors" with different backgrounds and customs, nearly every ethnic group, including the former majority white population, becomes more concerned for its own survival. Demographic data clearly indicate that California's future is multilingual, multicultural, and multiracial. However, because of a variety of historical and social factors, those who currently vote are mostly white, older, and well-to-do. How the gaps between the "old" California and the "new" California will be closed is not yet known. The challenge is to *acculturate* and assimilate new arrivals without destroying their unique cultural identities and without sacrificing the gains of the American-born population. Part of the solution to this challenge is to provide resources for an outstanding educational system that can help people overcome language barriers, cultural stereotypes, and *ethnocentrism*, as well as teach the technological skills and critical thinking essential for success in today's competitive world.

Cultural diversity can enrich daily life through the mingling of music, food, art, language, and even love (one-sixth of all children born in California have parents whose ethnic backgrounds are different from each other),[8] or it can be used to divide communities and individuals. During periods when the economy is growing, the need to blame usually is reduced, and calls to block the borders and shut down the safety net are heard less frequently. However, it is in the hard times, when jobs are scarce and government revenues are reduced, that political leaders must show their skill and compassion by emphasizing social unity rather than divisive politics of blame. That ability to show compassion and emphasize social unity may increase as political leaders from diverse backgrounds enter the halls of leadership. One sign is the substantial increase in Latino political strength; perhaps that community will set the example for the growing Asian groups. Clearly, all ethnic groups must work toward the common goals of all Californians, rather than emphasize a racially focused, divisive approach to the state's problems.

Even as Californians struggle to figure out how to live in the most multicultural state in the nation, other problems must not be forgotten. The state's ecosystem continues to require attention even during periods when environmental problems are not in the headlines. Debates over the proper management of California's magnificent natural resources involve numerous special-interest groups as well as many concerned individuals. The continuing destruction of agricultural land to meet the housing and shopping needs of a growing population (see Figure 15.2), the unresolved battles over water supplies, the battles over where to dump the inevitable toxic wastes of a chemically dependent economy, and the debates over energy resources all contribute to the long list of vital issues that must be faced by elected officials and the public. With little publicity, environmental battles are constantly fought. The skirmishes take place in legislative committees, at community meetings, and at environmentally sensitive sites throughout the state.

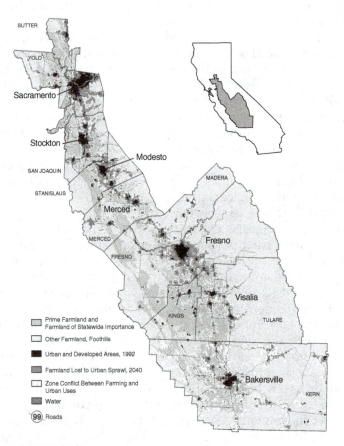

FIGURE 15.2 **California's Central Valley: Urban Sprawl by 2040**

Source: American Farmland Trust, *Alternatives for Future Urban Growth in California's Central Valley*, October 1995, http://www.farmlandinfo.org/ documents/30361/FUTURE_URBAN_GROWTH_IN_CALIFORNIAS_ CENTRAL_VALLEY.pdf

In addition to those issues already mentioned, other problems include how to clean up the beaches and bays, how much pesticides can be tolerated on our farms and on our food, how ancient forests can be preserved, where nuclear plants or oil derricks can be built, and, in general, how to balance the needs of nature with the needs of the 38 million human beings in the state. The state's environmental progress is also heavily impacted by federal decisions in matters regarding vehicle mileage and emissions standards, water regulations, access to offshore oil drilling, and other environmental matters primarily controlled by federal politics.

Although not every Californian is equally concerned about environmental issues, it is the underrepresented ethnic groups who often shoulder the burden of environmental damage. Many of the state's toxic waste dumps are located in minority communities, and rates of asthma and other respiratory diseases are worse in inner cities than in suburbs. Environmental justice movements include Latinos in the Central Valley and African Americans in South Los Angeles, using legal challenges as well as administrative procedures to state their claims.[9] The growing environmental concerns in communities of color include questions about lead residues in residential housing, water quality in urban areas, and asbestos in public facilities. While everyone tends to support a clean environment, the issue of who pays the cost of cleaning up our society's mess continues to be controversial.

IS CALIFORNIA GOVERNABLE?

Facing such enormous challenges, California needs good political leadership more than ever. Deciding how to respond to national and global economic changes, integrate the increasingly diverse population, provide adequate education and other services to all Californians, regulate business enough to protect people and their environment yet keep corporations from leaving the state, protect irreplaceable natural resources—all of these tasks face a divided state government, which often appears most concerned about its own perks and privileges. Divisions abound—within the parties and between them, between a multitude of ethnic and cultural communities, and among the many special-interest groups that manipulate so much of the decision-making process.

Until each of us recognizes the unique opportunities of the state and joins with other concerned citizens to right the existing wrongs, it may well be that the Golden State will never again fully reflect the historic California Dream. That would be a profound disservice to the Californians of today and those of tomorrow. We can only hope that Californians will pull together to avoid this tragic outcome. Californians of all backgrounds must strive to ensure that all ethnic and cultural groups participate and that all elected officials increase their responsiveness to the public (and perhaps reduce their level of service to narrow special-interest groups).

No one group can dominate in a state that no longer has a single majority group. It will be the responsibility of the most educated and concerned members of every group to mobilize their friends and associates to join in active, organized efforts to improve life in California.

Unless the general public understands these challenges and the individual's role in them, the future will never be as golden as the state's historic promise. Everyone, to varying degrees, uses the services provided through our state and local governments: airports, highways, beaches, schools, disability checks, community college classes, libraries, drivers licenses, professional licenses, county hospitals—the list is endless. All of us must remember that these services require public money that must be allocated carefully and spent wisely. Those who protest endlessly about paying their share must remember the part of the American ethic which says "United we stand, divided we fall." No Californian can be an island; each and every one must share the benefits and pay for the costs of life in California, the cutting edge of the nation.

QUESTIONS TO CONSIDER

Using Your Text and Your Own Experiences

1. What are some of the strengths and weaknesses of today's economy? What can the state government do to enhance the economic well-being of the state's people? Should government be involved in promoting economic well-being?

2. What are some strengths and weaknesses of California's political and social circumstances? Who benefits and who loses in the current system? How are you affected by this situation?

3. What can you do to make California a better place to live?

ENJOYING MEDIA

Movies to See and Web sites to Explore

California High Speed Rail Authority   cahighspeedrail.ca.gov
The agency charged with planning, designing, constructing, and operating a state-of-the-art high-speed train system with trains moving at 220 mph linking San Diego to San Francisco. (The funds for building this project are not yet determined.)

California Fuel Cell Partnership   cafcp.org
A collaboration of 31 organizations that believe fuel cell vehicles powered by hydrogen have the potential to change the future of transportation. The Web site presents the progress that CaFCP's automotive, energy, fuel cell technology, government, and associate members are making to bring this important transportation choice to market.

Future Problem Solving Program of California   cafpsp.org
An academic program for students in grades 4–12 designed to foster interest in the future and societal issues that will impact the lives of today's students.

Who Killed the Electric Car? Chris Paine, 2006
A documentary film that explores the birth, limited commercialization, and subsequent death of the battery electric vehicle in the United States, specifically the General Motors EV1 of the 1990s. California is among the states that have strong policies to encourage alternative vehicles in order to reduce emissions, greenhouse gases, and global warming.

King of California, Mike Cahill, 2007
In this lopsided view of California suburban life, a mentally unstable dad convinces his teen daughter to help him dig for Spanish-era gold under the local Costco. Reveals some of the idiosyncracies of contemporary California consumer culture, the facelessness of public bureaucracy, and issues of land development as big box shopping chains take over the countryside.

ENDNOTES

1. California Labor Market Info, California Employment Development Department, July 2009. http://www.labormarketinfo.edd.ca.gov.
2. Mark Baldassare, Dean Bonner, Jennifer Paluch, and Sonja Petek, "PPIC Statewide Survey: Californians and the Environment," Public Policy Institute of California, July 2009, http://www.ppic.org/content/pubs/survey/S_709MBS.pdf.
3. Labor Market Info, California Employment Development Department, July 2009. http://www.labormarketinfo.edd.ca.gov/cgi/databrowsing/localArea ProfileQSResults.asp?selectedarea=California&selectedindex=0&menuChoice= localAreaPro&state=true&geogArea=0601000000&countyName=.
4. Olivia Calderon, "2009 California Legislative Agenda of the Asset Building Program," New American Foundation, April 2, 2009. http://www.newamerica. net/publications/policy/2009_california_legislative_agenda_asset_building_ program.
5. Jed Kelko, David Neumark, and Marisol Cuellar Mejia, "Business Climate Rankings and the California Economy," Public Policy Institute of California, April 2011. http://www.ppic.org/content/pubs/report/R_411JKR.pdf.
6. Labor Market Info, California Employment Development Department, 2009.
7. Hans Johnson, "Educating California: Choices for the Future," Public Policy Institute of California, 2009, p. 3.
8. Bettina Boxall and Ray F. Herndon, "Far from Urban Gateways, Racial Lines Blur in Suburbs," *Los Angeles Times*, August 15, 2000, p. A1.
9. Ashlie Rodriguez, EPA Sued Over Toxic Waste Dumps in California, *Los Angeles Times*, July 7, 2011. http://www.latimes.com/news/local/ la-me-dumps-suit-20110707,0,7682583.story.

Directory of Political Organizations That Anyone Can Join

American Independent Party (conservative minor party)
1084 W. Marshall Blvd.
San Bernardino, CA 92405
http://www.aipca.org

Anti-Defamation League (antidiscrimination, antibigotry)
http://www.adl.org

Asian Pacific American Legal Center (civil rights issues)
231 E. Third Street
Los Angeles, CA 90013
http://www.apanet.org

California Public Interest Research Group (CALPIRG) (consumer and environmental issues)
3435 Wilshire #308
Los Angeles, CA 90010
http://www.calpirg.org

California Rural Legal Assistance Fund (legal help in rural areas)
Locations throughout California.
http://www.crla.org

California Tomorrow (making diversity work/children's issues)
436 14th Street,
Oakland, CA 94612
http://www.californiatomorrow.org

California Voter Foundation (using the Web to be informed)
2401 L St.
Sacramento, CA 95816
http://www.calvoter.org

Children Now—California (children's health, education, etc.)
1212 Broadway, 5th floor
Oakland, CA 94612
http://www.childrennow.org

Coalition for Clean Air (air quality issues)
Offices in Sacramento, Los Angeles, Fresno
http://www.coalitionforcleanair.org

Coalition for Economic Survival (tenants' rights)
514 Shatto Place
Los Angeles, CA 90020
http://www.cesinaction.org

Common Cause (quality of government issues)
http://www.commoncause.org

Democratic Party of California (partisan)
http://www.cadem.org

Gay and Lesbian Alliance Against Defamation (monitoring homophobia in media)
5455 Wilshire Blvd, #1500
Los Angeles, CA 90036
http://www.glaad.org

Green Party (environmental justice/nonviolence)
http://www.cagreens.org

Handgun Control Inc. (gun control lobby)
703 Market St. #1511
San Francisco, CA 94103
http://www.handguncontrol.org

Health Access (affordable health care for Californians)
942 Market St. #402
San Francisco, CA 94102
http://www.health-access.org

Japanese American Citizens League (civil rights)
1765 Sutter Street
San Francisco, CA 94115
http://www.jacl.org

Labor/Community Strategy Center (environmental/social justice)
3780 Wilshire Blvd., Suite 1200
Los Angeles, CA 90010
http://www.thestrategycenter.org

League of Conservation Voters—California (environmental)
350 Frank Ogawa Plaza
Oakland, CA 94612
http://www.ecovote.org

League of Women Voters of California (nonpartisan political reform issues)
926 J St. #515
Sacramento, CA 95814
http://www.lwv.org

Libertarian Party of California (antigovernment minor party)
655 Lewelling Blvd., Suite 362
San Leandro, CA 94579
http://www.lp.org

Mexican American Legal Defense and Education Foundation (civil rights)
634 S. Spring Street
Los Angeles, CA 90014
http://www.maldef.org

National Association for the Advancement of Colored People (one of the first civil rights groups)
3910 W. Martin Luther King Jr. Blvd.
Los Angeles, CA 90008
http://www.naacp.org

National Organization for Women (women's issues)
926 J St. #523
Sacramento, CA 95814
http://www.canow.org

Planned Parenthood of California (family planning lobby)
555 Capitol Mall
Sacramento, CA 95816
http://www.ppactionca.org

Planning and Conservation League (environmental issues)
1107, 9th Street
Sacramento, CA 95814
http://www.pcl.org

Republican Party of California (partisan)
1903 W. Magnolia Blvd.
Burbank, CA 91505
http://www.cagop.org

Sierra Club (environmental issues)
85 Second Street
San Francisco, CA 94105
http://www.sierraclub.org

Southern California Library for Social Studies and Research (social movement documents/ conferences)
6120 S. Vermont Ave.
Los Angeles, CA 90044
http://www.socallib.org

Southwest Voter Research/William C. Velasquez Institute (encourage Latino voting and political action)
2914 N. Main St., 2nd floor
Los Angeles, CA 90031
800-222-5654
http://www.svrep.org

Traditional Values Group (conservative Christian lobby)
100 S. Anaheim Blvd
Anaheim, CA 92805
http://www.traditionalvalues.org

The Utility Reform Network (TURN) (consumer advocacy)
115 Sansome Street
San Francisco, CA 94104
http://www.turn.org

Communicating Your Views to Your Elected Officials

Since every Californian is represented by multiple elected officials, it can be confusing to find the one you need. Each of us has two U.S. senators, one U.S. House of Representatives member, one state senator, and one Assembly member, as well as eight state constitutional officers (including the governor). Then at the local level, you have a county supervisor, city council representative(s) (unless you live in an unincorporated area), and numerous school board and community college board representatives.

HOW CAN YOU FIND THE PERSON YOU NEED?

1. Analyze the situation. Do you need a local, state, or federal response? If you wish to express your views on legislation, make sure you know whether it originated in Washington, D.C., Sacramento, or your city hall. Get the bill number and author's name.

2. There are several ways to find out who represents you at each level of government. The best is probably the Internet. You may also find listings in your local telephone directory in a section for Government.
   Useful Web sites for finding your representatives at different levels of government:
   http://www.senate.ca.gov
   http://www.assembly.ca.gov
   http://www.house.gov/writerep/
   http://thomas.loc.gov/

3. You may use e-mail, telephone calls, and/or "snail mail" letters to communicate with your elected officials. You may also request an appointment (especially if you are part of a group) and you have the right to appear before a public body to speak to them. And, as an American, you also have the right to peaceably assemble to protest, such as the many Occupy protests that took place in 2011.

Use your own words to briefly describe your problem, concern, or question. If you are expressing your views about specific legislation, refer to the bill number and author's name. Be brief and constructive in your comments. Explain your reasons for your views on the issue.

Be sure to include your full name and address, even if you send an e-mail. Elected officials want to know if you are their constituent; some of them will respond to letters, depending upon the volume of mail and whether they have adequate staff.

Acculturate The process by which immigrants learn their new culture's language, customs, and traditions.

Affirmative action A policy designed to enhance opportunities for ethnic or other groups who were denied access in the past, such as African Americans and Latinos.

Amend To change a document such as a bill.

Appropriations Funds allocated by elected officials for public programs.

Assimilation The process by which a new group learns the rules of the more-established group and adopts its customs.

At-large A method of electing members of a city council or other legislative body by voters in the entire governmental unit rather than in individual districts.

Ballot initiative See **Initiative**.

Ballot status Appearing on the ballot, such as a political party.

Baseline budget A budget based on the previous year's budget rather than a "zero-based" budget that requires all programs to justify their existence.

Bond measures Ballot measures that require voter approval so that the state or local governments may borrow money for land purchases and construction investments (prisons, schools, roads, parks, etc.). Bonds may not be used for operating costs.

Bracero A legal temporary immigrant worker usually brought from Mexico to work in agriculture.

By district Elections held in sub-districts or wards of a political jurisdiction, for example, a city council in which each elected member represents a geographic area within the city. Such districts must be roughly equal in population.

Californios Residents of California who were of Mexican descent during the period following Mexico's loss of California to the United States (1848–1890s).

Challenger In politics, a person who runs against an incumbent.

Charter school A public school that operates under a charter agreement which enables it to function without adhering to all of the standard state and local regulations.

Civil liberties Protected types of behavior such as freedom of speech or religion, which governments are prohibited from taking away.

Civil rights Legally imposed obligations, such as the right to equal protection of the laws or reasonable bail, that governments owe to individuals.

Civil service system A set of procedures for hiring government employees on the basis of merit, usually demonstrated by examination, and protecting them against unjust firing.

Class gap An increasing gap in resources between the wealthiest and the poorest people.

Closed primary A primary (first) election in which only voters who are members of a specific political party may vote for that party's candidates.

Conference committee A temporary committee appointed to resolve differences between the Senate and Assembly versions of a bill.

Conquistadores Spanish conquerors in the New World (Western Hemisphere).

Conservative A political philosophy that favors smaller government, lower taxes, fewer public services, and a "laissez-faire" (let them do as they please) approach to business.

Constitutional offices The executive offices that the state constitution requires must be elected by the voters.

Contract city City that purchases police and fire services from the county.

Council–manager A form of city government in which the elected city council, with legislative authority, appoints, and can fire, a city manager to whom the various executive departments are responsible.

County committee Also known as county central committee; a group of elected party activists within each county.

Decline to state A voter's registration status when he or she does not wish to affiliate with any political party.

Defendant In a civil case, the entity being sued; in a criminal case, the accused person.

Demographic shift Noticeable changes in population data, including number of people, size of ethnic groups, and so on.

Direct democracy The reforms of the Progressive movement, which enable voters to directly make laws, amend the state constitution, recall officials, or repeal laws passed by elected representatives.

District-based A city, school district, or other governmental unit is divided into geographic districts, each of which has a representative elected by the voters in that district.

Electoral votes The number of votes a state may cast in electing the president and vice president, computed by adding the number of its U.S. senators (2) to the number of Representatives (53 for California as of 2000).

Electorate Those who vote.

Ethnocentrism The belief that one's own ethnic group is superior to other ethnic groups.

Executive clemency The governor's power to lighten criminal sentences imposed by the courts by pardons, which cancel them, commutations, which reduce them, or reprieves, which postpone them; amnesties are pardons for an entire group.

Ex-officio A nonvoting member of a governmental body.

Federalism A political system in which the national and state systems have some powers independent of each other.

Felonies The most serious crimes, including murder, rape, and arson.

Franchise In politics, the right to vote.

Gerrymandering Manipulation of district boundaries to favor the election of a particular group, individual, or candidate of the dominant political party.

GLBT An acronym for gay, lesbian, bisexual, and transgender.

Globalization The increasing economic interdependence of many nations.

Grassroots Pertaining to actions, movements, or organizations of a political nature that rely chiefly on the mass involvement of ordinary citizens.

Gubernatorial Pertaining to the office of governor.

Image making Creating a positive impression about a candidate through the use of public relations methods and mass media.

Incumbent Person currently in office.

Independent expenditure Campaign spending by a person or organization that does not coordinate such spending with the candidate.

Indictment Formal accusation of criminal behavior by a grand jury, sometimes used to bring defendants to trial.

Inflation A situation in which prices increase rapidly.

Infractions Minor criminal offenses, such as jaywalking.

Infrastructure The tangible components that allow society to function; bridges, roads, water systems, sewage systems, and so on.

Initiative The process by which citizens can propose a state or local law or amendment to the state constitution by signing a formal petition asking that it be submitted as a ballot proposition for voter approval.

Interest groups See **Special-interest groups.**

Issue-oriented organizations Groups concerned primarily with political issues, such as abortion, civil rights, medical care, and so forth, as opposed to groups interested in electing specific candidates.

Item veto Sometimes called the line-item veto; the authority of the governor to reduce or eliminate money appropriated by the legislature for a specific purpose while signing the remaining provisions of the bill into law.

Liberal A political philosophy that supports active government involvement in creating a more just society and that supports individual freedom in personal matters.

Lobbying The attempt to influence government policy, usually on behalf of an interest group.

Majority More than 50 percent.

Mandates Requirements: for example, a federal mandate may require states to take a particular action.

Manifest destiny The justification of U.S. territorial expansion based on the mystical assumption that it was the clear fate of the nation to acquire at least all land between the Atlantic and Pacific oceans.

Mayor–council A form of city government based on a separation of powers between a mayor with executive authority and the council with legislative authority, both elected by the voters.

Mestizo Of mixed race, particularly Spanish European and pre-Columbian Indian heritage.

Minimalist That which is limited to its simplest or most essential elements; politically, the usually conservative belief that government should do very little.

Misdemeanors An intermediate level of crime, less damaging to persons or property than a felony.

Monocultural electorate A term that describes California's largely white electorate, in contrast to a largely nonwhite population at large.

Multi-issue regional agency Agency that coordinates tasks and plans of all the various local government units in a region, typically in an advisory capacity.

Naturalization The process of becoming a U.S. citizen.

Nonpartisan (elections) Elections, such as those of judges, school board members, and city and county officials in California, in which the party affiliation of the candidates does not appear on the ballot.

Office-block ballot To discourage straight-ticket party voting, the arrangement of candidates' names according to the office for which they are running rather than their party affiliation.

Ordinance A law passed by a city or county.

Out of the closet Open about one's gay or lesbian sexual orientation.

Outsourcing The movement of work outside the state or nation, such as customer service phone calls or the production of goods.

Override When the legislative body votes again on a bill vetoed by the executive and overcomes the veto by a two-thirds majority so that the bill becomes law without the executive's approval.

Partisan Reflecting strong loyalty to a party or political faction.

Partisan election An election in which the party affiliation of the candidates appears on the ballot.

Party affiliation An individual's choice of a party when registering to vote; may or may not include any activity in that party.

Patronage The use of appointment powers to reward political supporters.

Plaintiff The person bringing suit in a civil case.

Plea bargain Negotiations in a criminal case designed to get the defendant to plead guilty if the prosecution reduces the seriousness of the charge or reduces the sentence.

Plurality The most votes.

Polarization A sharp division between groups, such as the increasing differences in views between conservative Republicans and liberal Democrats.

Political action committee (PAC) An organization, usually formed by an interest group or corporation, designed to solicit money from individuals to be used for campaign contributions to candidates endorsed by the group.

Polls The location where votes are cast; in opinion research, surveys of public opinion.

President pro tem The leader of the state Senate, elected by the membership.

Private sector Refers to all business and other activities that are not sponsored directly by government; however, much of the American private sector is subsidized through government funds.

Privatization Any effort to cut back government and substitute private-sector activity; for example, firing public janitors and "contracting out" to a private profit-seeking janitorial service.

Progressive movement The growing demand in the early 1900s for direct democracy options such as initiative, recall, and referendum.

Proposition An item on the ballot that requires a "yes" or "no" vote, including initiative, referendum, recall, and bond issue.

Recall A progressive era reform permitting the voters, by petition, to call a special election to remove an official from office before the next regularly scheduled election.

Recession A period during which the economy slows down, including fewer jobs, higher unemployment, lower consumption, and reduced tax revenues.

Redbaiting During the Cold War, the effort to discredit a person by implying that he or she was a communist ("red").

Redistricting Redrawing the boundaries of election districts; required after each census to keep district populations as nearly equal as possible.

Referendum The type of ballot proposition that allows voters to repeal or revoke laws passed by the legislature.

Regressive In reference to taxation, indicates that the poor are taxed more than the rich in proportion to their incomes.

Repatriation Returning immigrants to their country of origin.

Representative democracy System in which citizens elect representatives to make decisions.

Runaway production When films are produced outside California, leading to job loss in the state's entertainment industry.

Runoff election An election held when no candidate in a nonpartisan primary receives a majority; the two top candidates enter the "runoff" so that the final winner is elected by a majority vote.

Scapegoating The process of blaming a social/ethnic group for society's problems.

Service industry An industry that does not manufacture anything but rather provides services, such as health care, education, or retail sales.

Settlement Money awarded to a plaintiff through negotiations.

Single-issue regional agency A large special district that provides a service or regulates an area, such as air quality or water supplies.

Speaker of the assembly The presiding officer and most powerful member of the Assembly, elected by the membership.

Special district Local units of government which perform a service that no city or county provides, which may encompass an area larger than any one city or county, and which have their own governing body, either appointed or elected.

Special-interest groups Also known as pressure groups or lobbies; organizations that try to influence politicians to achieve their political and economic aims.

Standing committees Permanent committees of the California Senate and Assembly organized around policy subjects, to which every bill is referred and in which most of the work of legislation occurs.

Statute A law that is in the code books and is not part of an actual constitution or charter.

Swing votes Votes that are not predictable and can be swayed to support candidates or issues.

Target audience A select group of voters who receive political mailings with messages aimed at winning their support.

Tax assessment In reference to property taxes, the amount that must be paid; it is based upon the property's assessed value.

Term limits A rule that permits a politician only a limited number of opportunities to run for the same office. Term limits exist at the state level and in some cities in California.

Two-tier society A society in which there is a small affluent upper class, a large class of impoverished people, including the working poor and the underclass, and a small middle class.

Unaffiliated A voter who chooses no political party when registering to vote.

Underclass Those long-term impoverished persons who survive through government assistance, charity, or criminal activity. They should not be confused with the "working poor," although income levels may be similar.

Underrepresented Ethnic or other groups that have historically not had political representation in proportion to their population.

Unincorporated area Territory outside the boundaries of incorporated cities whose residents receive nearly all municipal services from county government.

Unitary In contrast to a federal system, one in which the county and other regional or local governments have only the powers the state gives to them.

Veto The return of a bill by the chief executive to the legislative body that passed it, unsigned, thereby killing it unless the legislature overrides the veto.

Vote-by-mail (VBM) An option available to all voters to request a VBM ballot, vote and mail it, and avoid going in person to the polling place on election day.

White flight The process by which whites move away from areas as ethnic minorities begin to move in.

Arax, Mark, *West of the West: Dreamers, Believers, Builders, and Killers in the Golden State*, Public Affairs, New York, 2009.

Baldassare, Mark, *A California State of Mind: The Conflicted Voter in a Changing World*, University of California Press, 2002.

Beebe, Rose Marie, and Robert Senkewicz, *Chronicles of Early California: Lands of Promise and Despair, 1535–1846*, Heyday Books, 2001.

Brechin, Gray, *Imperial San Francisco: Urban Power, Earthly Ruin*, University of California Press, 1999.

Erie, Steven P, *Beyond Chinatown: The Metropolitan Water District, Growth, and the Environment in Southern California*, Stanford University Press, 2006.

Flamming, Douglas, *Bound for Freedom: Black Los Angeles in Jim Crow America*, University of California Press, 2005.

Fradkin, Philip, *The Seven States of California: A Natural and Human History*, University of California Press, 1999.

Glantz, Stanton A., and Edith Balbach, *Tobacco War: Inside the California Battle*, University of California Press, 2000.

Gordon, Bernard, *Hollywood Exile or How I Learned to Love the Blacklist*, University of Texas Press, 2000.

Gumprecht, Blake, *The Los Angeles River: Its Life, Death and Possible Rebirth*, Johns Hopkins University Press, 1999.

Gutierrez, Ramon A., and Richard Orsi, *Contested Eden: California Before the Gold Rush*, University of California Press, 1998.

Hanak, Ellen, et al., *California 2025: Taking on the Future*, Public Policy Institute, 2005.

Haslam, Gerald, *Workin' Man Blues: Country Music in California*, University of California Press, 1999.

Hayes-Bautista, David, *La Nueva California: Latinos in the Golden State*, University of California Press, 2004.

Hise, Greg, and William Deverell, *Eden by Design: The 1930 Olmsted-Bartholomew Plan for the Los Angeles Region*, University of California Press, 2000.

Hurewitz, Daniel, *Bohemian Los Angeles and the Making of Modern Politics*, University of California Press, 2007.

Lubenow, Gerald, *California Votes: The 2002 Governor's Race and the Recall that Made History*, Berkeley Public Policy Press, Institute of Governmental Studies, 2003.

Martinez, Ruben, *Crossing Over: A Mexican Family on the Migrant Trail*, Metropolitan Books, 2001.

McClung, Sue, *Water and the Shaping of California*, Water Education Foundation, 2000.

McClung, William Alexander, *Landscapes of Desire: Anglo Mythologies of Los Angeles*, University of California Press, 2000.

Merchant, Carolyn, *Green Versus Gold: Sources in California's Environmental History*, Island Press, 1998.

Michael, Jay, and Dan Walters, *The Third House: Lobbyists, Money and Power in Sacramento*, University of California Press, 2002.

Mulholland, Catherine, *William Mulholland and the Rise of Los Angeles*, University of California Press, 2000.

Myers, Dowell, *Immigrants and Boomers: Forging a New Social Contract for the Future of America*, Russell Sage Foundation, 2006.

Ochoa, Enrique C., and Gilda L. Ochoa, *Latino Los Angeles: Transformations, Communities, and Activism*, University of Arizona Press, 2005.

Pincetl, Stephanie, *Transforming California: A Political History of Land Use and Development*, Johns Hopkins University Press, 1999.

Pitti, Stephen, *The Devil in Silicon Valley: Northern California, Race and Mexican Americans*, Princeton University Press, 2003.

Reed, Deborah, et al., *Educational Progress across Immigrant Generations in California*, Public Policy Institute, 2005.

Roderick, Kevin, *The San Fernando Valley: America's Suburb*, Los Angeles Times Books, 2001.

Schiesl, Martin, and Mark Dodge, *City of Promise: Race and Historical Change in Los Angeles*, Regina Books, 2006.

Schwartz, Stephen, *From West to East: California and the Making of the American Mind*, Free Press, 1998.

Secrest, William, *When the Great Spirit Died: The Destruction of the California Indians, 1850–1860*, Word Dancer Press, 2003.

Starrs, Paul F., *A Field Guide to California Agriculture*, UC Berkeley Press, 2010.

Yung, Judy, *Unbound Voices: A Documentary History of Chinese Women in San Francisco*, University of California Press, 1999.

Note: The letters 'f' and 't' following the locators refer to figures and tables respectively.